Helen Co
£5
CW00546624

Setting Up Your Ceramic Studio

Ideas & Plans from Working Artists

Setting Up Your Ceramic Studio

Ideas & Plans from Working Artists

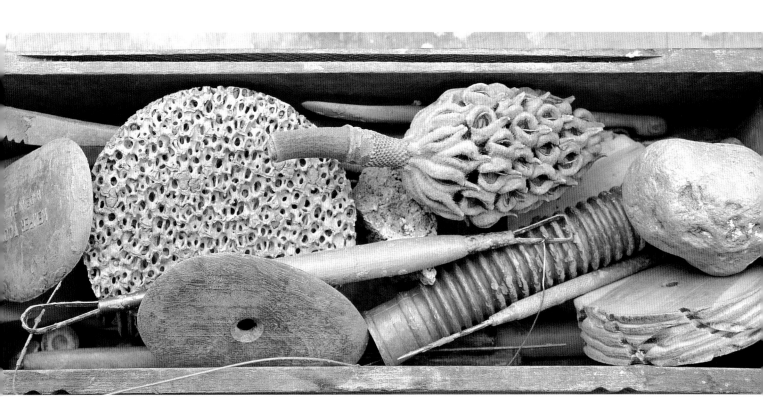

Virginia Scotchie

LARK BOOKS

A Division of Sterling Publishing Co., Inc.
New York

EDITOR
Suzanne J. E. Tourtillott

ART DIRECTOR
Susan McBride

ASSISTANT ART DIRECTOR
Hannes Charen

PHOTOGRAPHER
David H. Ramsey

COVER DESIGN
Barbara Zaretsky

ILLUSTRATOR
Olivier Rollin

ASSISTANT EDITOR
Veronika Alice Gunter

EDITORIAL ASSISTANCE
Anne Wolff Hollyfield
Delores Gosnell

PRODUCTION ASSISTANCE
Shannon Yokeley

Library of Congress has cataloged the hardcover edition as follows:

Scotchie, Virginia.
  Setting up your ceramic studio: ideas & plans from working artists /
Virginia Scotchie.
     p. cm.
Includes index.
  ISBN 1-57990-422-X
  1. Artists' studios--Design and construction. 2. Pottery
craft--Vocational guidance. 3. Pottery industry--United
States--Management. 4. Small business--United States--Management. I.
Title.
  N8520.S36 2003
  738'.068--dc21

                                                    2003005194

10 9 8 7 6 5 4 3 2 1

Published by Lark Books, a division of
Sterling Publishing Co., Inc.
387 Park Avenue South, New York, N.Y. 10016

First Paperback Edition 2005
© 2003, Virginia Scotchie

Distributed in Canada by Sterling Publishing,
c/o Canadian Manda Group, 165 Dufferin Street
Toronto, Ontario, Canada M6K 3H6

Distributed in the U.K. by Guild of Master Craftsman Publications Ltd.
Castle Place, 166 High Street, Lewes, East Sussex, England BN7 1XU
Tel: (+ 44) 1273 477374, Fax: (+ 44) 1273 478606
Email: pubs@thegmcgroup.com, Web: www.gmcpublications.com

Distributed in Australia by Capricorn Link (Australia) Pty Ltd.
P.O. Box 704, Windsor, NSW 2756 Australia

The written instructions, photographs, designs, patterns, and projects in this volume are intended for the personal use of the reader and may be reproduced for that purpose only. Any other use, especially commercial use, is forbidden under law without written permission of the copyright holder.

Every effort has been made to ensure that all the information in this book is accurate. However, due to differing conditions, tools, and individual skills, the publisher cannot be responsible for any injuries, losses, and other damages that may result from the use of the information in this book.

If you have questions or comments about this book, please contact:
Lark Books
67 Broadway
Asheville, NC 28801
(828) 253-0467

Manufactured in China

All rights reserved

ISBN 1-57990-422-x (hardcover) 1-57990-672-9 (paperback)

Contents

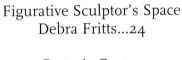
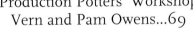
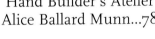
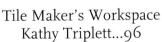

Ben Owen III's studio

INTRODUCTION

The old adage says that art can be made anywhere. But however true this may be, the fact is we all dream of the perfect studio. This book will take you through the studios of 12 ceramic artists who, in their unique way, created dream studios in which they work and live. These spaces are as varied and particular as the ceramic work itself. They are magical chambers that serve as the arena where the artist's vision materializes from the clay. If an artist's work fascinates me, I wonder how it evolved. What personal elements went into a piece? What are its technical aspects, and where was it made? I've always experienced a sense of excitement and curiosity as I enter an artist's studio, because there I can gain insight into his or her world.

Many of these studios are located in the southeastern United States. Their designs range from rustic and rural, as shown on this page, to the spare and contemporary style at left. They serve as an archive of their owners' methods, interests, dreams, and inspirations, and a visit can give you a fresh perspective on creativity and the basis for a new kind of understanding. The look and feel of a studio constantly shapes the art conceived of and created within its wall.

Each studio functions in a singular way, with its special stock of tools, materials, and sources of inspiration. These make up the secret essences and formulas that account for so much of the power of an image or form. This is the space in which the artist can step away from the rest of the world and create, a space that embodies the heart and soul of the artistic process.

Pam and Vern Owens' Jugtown Pottery

Michael Sherrill's studio

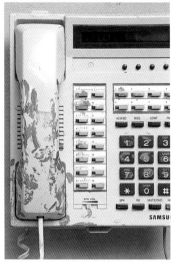

The studios presented here are visually documented to give a sense of their interior and exterior spaces, as well as the hidden nooks and crannies where glaze brushes are hung, glaze tests are stored, and ephemera shine forth. Often these are private spaces where no one but the artist may enter. She alone knows where a particular tool is kept or how it is used. Though furnished with the most ordinary objects, the work space has an aura of mystery and excitement.

The most important thing that the ceramic artist must focus on is that she must keep making her work. But where? And how? Yes, art can be made anywhere, but the fact remains that working in ceramics requires a few basic supplies and tools. One featured ceramic artist said a good strong wooden table is the most important studio item with which to begin work. One could argue that all you need is a floor to pound the clay on. Of course, if you create work on a potter's wheel, that may be the most important tool. Many artists cart bone-dry work to a friend's kiln or to a community art center to fire, so an electric kiln might be the next indispensable item.

Debra Fritts' studio courtyard

In this book you'll discover how a ceramic artist can assemble a studio, starting with the basic needs for equipment, lighting, and ventilation, including details of the various ways these artists have solved problems with heating and cooling, storage, and glazing and firing spaces.

This book is a journey that looks in on inventive ceramic artists who have not only established a place for themselves through their creations, but also have created studios that are exciting and vibrant places to make their work. The layout and design of each studio and what these interiors hold reflect the art produced there. History has proven the clay process to be nearly eternal, but in many ways the ceramic artist's studio has changed as much as the world of ceramic art itself.

Many ceramic studios are a part of a rural community.

THE FUNDAMENTAL
Studio

REALIZE THE SPACE

Potters, ceramists, and amateur clay artists of every stripe practically live in their studios—or wish they could. Creating a new studio (whether it's your first or fifth) can be both a daunting prospect and an exhilarating project, because there are plenty of practical matters to consider before your vision can become reality. Even if you're not planning to build the perfect studio, your converted-garage work space or backyard shed might benefit from an overhaul. After all, working in the most efficient, inspiring clay space possible may well be a catalyst for new insight and creativity.

A scenic view contributes to the creative process.

Draw the Big Picture

The planning phase can feel like facing a giant sheet of blank paper. You know you'll be making many decisions along the way, but where to start? No matter if you're contemplating an original design, a renovation, or a relocation, available square footage and its close companion, money, will be the most limiting (or liberating) factors. And how much of either commodity is necessary depends on the importance you place on the basics of life in the studio: space, light, equipment, utilities, and access.

Focus on what conditions you feel are necessary for your work and how they will intertwine in the studio. What conditions might best promote your artistic and commercial goals? Would acres of work surface help you better execute big projects? Do you want lots of natural light because it energizes you? Could shelving right next to the wheel help you stay more focused on throwing? These questions will help you sketch the broad outlines. You're on your way to making those important early decisions about where and how to create a studio that works well.

Situate the Studio

Before renting, relocating, or building a studio, consider location and accessibility. Would you accomplish more if your studio were in your backyard or close to where you live, rather than in the next county or in an urban location where parking is at a premium? Tranquil views may leave you feeling isolated and lonely unless you're part of a supportive community of artists. An urban studio is more stimulating, with access to other artists and influences, but it may pose problems—both logistic and regulatory—for certain types of equipment, especially kilns.

The climate and terrain of the region may limit or expand your options for heating, cooling, and other practical considerations. Artists who live in more extreme climates may have to weigh the benefits of large windows and a generous floor plan against their resulting cost increases.

Even if the ideal location isn't possible, you'll still have plenty of opportunity for choices and decisions within your studio's four walls. Once you give these fundamentals some careful thought, you can plan a steady, harmonious work flow.

Create Flow

In the ceramic process, mind, body, and space function together in a deliberate way. Their unity is vital. The clay demands intensive work and many steps along the way, and effective work flow ensures that you'll be able to move from one stage in the process to another with relative ease. You shouldn't have to move glaze buckets to reach the kiln. The most efficient clay studios, no matter how small or large, have task-specific areas, but a production pottery has a much different work flow than that of a figurative sculptor's studio. Potters must have space, mobility, and top efficiency; a sculptor may prefer an intimate or stripped-down space, minimizing distraction.

Workflow eases the labor-intensive ceramic process.

Most studios could use just a little more room. The simplest way to "gain" more space is to keep frequently used supplies, equipment, and tools close to the task area. Streamline any part of the process that will conserve your time and save your aching back. Repetitively moving the same heavy materials wastes motion and steals your energy. Keep the distances from the front door, over to the wedging or forming domain, and then on to the drying, glazing, and firing areas as short as possible—but be sure to allow wide aisles and enough space around the main worktable. A great way to facilitate the flow of work is to put equipment and tables on wheels. This is especially important in a high-volume studio, or in one with a lot of floor space. In Mike Vatalaro's glaze house, the ware carts, tables, clay mixer, and even some of his heavy power tools all roll and move with ease.

Enhance the Experience

Almost every ceramic studio has a unique spot where the artist at work feels most centered, one that is crucial to his or her creative process. This area best reflects the personality of the artist; some describe it as the heart and soul of their studio. The primary wheel or worktable, a collection of well-used tools and brushes, or perhaps a favorite old stool dwells here. Of particular importance to most of the artists I visited was the direction of natural light and a pleasing vista. Pets, too, seem to be as natural to studios as clay. For many of these ceramists, the connection to nature and wildlife directly impacts their work. The studios of Cynthia Bringle and Becky Gray, for example, include wonderful views of bird feeders, and the birds' activity adds a vibrant energy to the artists' lives in the studio.

The canvas-covered worktable is an essential part of the studio.

STUDIO REALITIES: SOFT & HARD WARE

If by design or necessity you want only the basics in your studio, some articles will be task specific, but others can do double duty (a slab roller easily transforms into a table). Potters usually put a low table near the wheel. A canvas-covered table works well for rolling coils or using slip to join clay forms, but an unfinished wooden or plastic-laminate surface is better for cutting slabs or using liquid applications, such as wax or glaze. Avoid polyurethane or other sealants on worktables, since they can cause clay to stick. Michael Sherrill carves his forms on salvaged industrial worktables that he fitted with new stainless steel tops.

Light delineates form and texture.

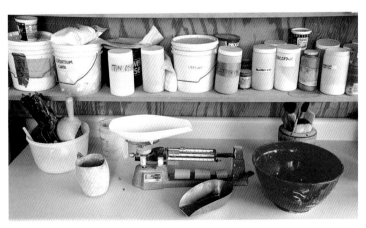

Use suitable surfaces for worktables.

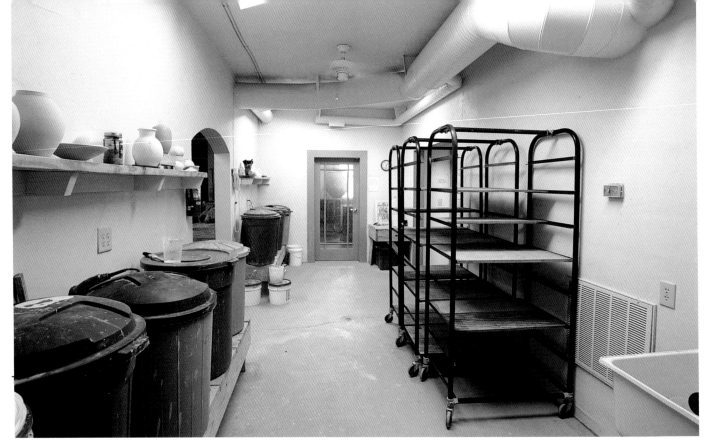

Task-specific areas use more space but ultimately streamline the work.

Adjustable, movable shelving, placed close to the action, makes it easy to store and move pieces of various sizes. I recommend that you invest in wheeled carts to hold the shelves—as many as the space and budget allow. Even if you don't move them often, at least you have the option. Designate separate carts for green ware, bisque, and glaze ware. Ware boards let you move a few wet, heavy pieces at a time to carts or shelves. To best utilize their two-person work space, as well as save steps, potters Kent McLaughlin and Suze Lindsay attached a pair of shelf brackets which hold a board to the front of their treadle and kick wheels.

Clay Ergonomics

Since we use our bodies to work with clay, it's crucial to follow ergonomic principles if we're to have a long life in the studio. Whether you're hand-building or throwing, glazing or packing work, the body must work intelligently. Ceramic artists typically suffer from back, knee, and wrist ailments that come from hours of bending, lifting, building, and throwing. There are many simple things you can do when planning your studio that will help to prevent unnecessary strain on your body. Don't carry that big bag of clay any farther than you need to! Roll it out of the storage area with a wheeled cart or dolly, or consider production potter Cynthia Bringle's clever solution: her brother installed a dumbwaiter in the two-story studio that brings bagged clay from the basement to the main level.

Another key factor in good back health is placement and height of tables (for standing work) and chairs (especially at the potter's wheel). Different body sizes and heights demand that you make whatever adjustments to the furniture that will help you maintain your best posture. Kent McLaughlin, for example, sits at his electric wheel in a wooden café-style chair that he blessed with shorter front legs so that his body tips forward slightly as he throws. For table work, use a stool with a back and a padded seat. Stand up, walk around, and stretch occasionally; prolonged periods of sitting make you stiff and uncomfortable. It's well worth the effort to stretch and release muscle tension.

Your studio floor also makes a big difference in how you feel at the end of the day. Many ceramists like a slightly sloped, sealed cement floor with a drain because it's so easy to hose down the day's clay dust regularly, but cement floors are hard on the legs. Use an antifatigue mat, available at restaurant supply stores, if you must stand for long periods, no matter what kind of flooring you have. Wooden floors are a popular alternative. This resilient material is easier on the back and legs than is stone or concrete.

HEALTH & SAFETY

Keeping a high standard of air quality is a concern for all ceramic artists. Constant exposure to clay dust is perhaps your greatest health hazard; dry clay, whether crushed underfoot, deposited as dust on shelves, or released during mixing, releases free silica into the air. Routinely clean your studio, learn how to properly handle raw clay materials, and ventilate and filter your ceramic and respiratory equipment—especially in the areas where you use powders or sprays. Always use personal protective equipment for your hair, eyes, skin, and lungs.

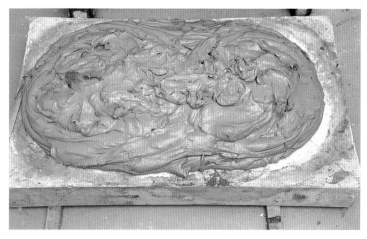

Recycled clay on a potter's plaster block

Air Quality

Because of the health risks from the powders and toxic fumes associated with ceramics, air quality is vitally important to the clay artist. To ensure that your studio is a healthful place, employ all three of these methods: room ventilation, local exhaust ventilation, and a respirator.

The respirator is essential for lung protection. There are two basic systems: filters trap airborne particulates released while you're mixing clay or spraying glazes, and cartridges capture vapors that escape from a hot kiln. Make sure that the seal fits your face well so that no outside air can be drawn into it. Periodically check and replace filters and cartridges, and store the mask in an airtight plastic bag.

Whenever possible, recycle clay scraps before they dry. Don't use a broom for clay dust; it's much better to use a damp sponge or mop, rinsing it into a bucket of water. If you must sweep your floors, use a commercial-grade, oiled sweeping compound to do so (though it takes a large quantity of the compound to do the job). Regular household and shop vacuums aren't equipped with the filtration system of a ceramic-studio vacuum—only a multifiltered studio vacuum can effectively capture the sub–micron-size particles that come from raw clay materials.

Use local-exhaust ventilation for a powder-mixing area, spray booth, and the kiln, and use adequate room ventilation, such as window exhaust plus a fresh (outdoor) air supply. Air conditioning won't provide the proper fresh air exchange.

All types of kilns pose some risks to health and environment.

Filtration & Sewage

Clay materials and their by-products can seriously clog sink and sewer pipes, so your drain should have a clay trap. When you need a sinkful of water, stand a short length of pipe in the drain so that only the cleanest water flows into it. Many artists rinse their hands and tools over a plastic bucket that captures the bulk of the clay before finishing the job in the sink. Certain glaze ingredients are toxic and must be stored, handled, and disposed of as hazardous waste, separate from nontoxic ceramic materials. Be a good neighbor: discard all solid waste you've collected in a manner consistent with your community's environmental-protection guidelines.

ILLUMINATION

All ceramists need and want plenty of wonderful light from windows and skylights, as well as task lights for rainy days and nighttime work. French doors and lots of windows let in the day at Debra Fritts's suburban studio. Mike Vatalaro positioned his electric wheel to one side of a large window because the angled morning light interacts with the form as he's throwing it, informing his creative process.

For even, consistent light, install long fluorescent tube lights on ceilings and beams. Commercial-quality tubes are now available with full-spectrum light that is important for better color rendition. Over time, your initial investment will pay off in energy savings. Mount clamp-on and track spotlights wherever you need task lighting for detail work. Clamping units hold either ordinary household bulbs or stronger, larger flood-style ones; follow the manufacturer's recommendations and use the proper bulb style and wattage.

ENERGY

Most ceramic artists find they need many electrical outlets in their studios for appliances such as task lights, hand mixers, and the stereo. Rather than rely on inconvenient (and potentially dangerous) extension cord schemes, plan or add outlets if the existing wiring will allow it. Fortunately, most electric potter's wheels require only a standard electrical plug, but you'll probably need sufficient power so that you can operate several pieces of electrical equipment simultaneously without causing power outages or surges.

Electric kilns need heavy-duty wiring that meets building codes.

Electric kilns and other heavy-duty equipment, such as clay mixers and pug mills, require special electrical outlets. First, determine whether the studio's power supply will safely and properly fire the kiln. Many electric kilns must be wired directly to an electrical box, not exceeding a maximum distance from it. In the United States, single-phase household current is rated at 220/240 volts, but educational institutions, industrial facilities, and commercial buildings are often supplied with 208 volts and three-phase wiring. If the kiln isn't correctly matched to its power source, it will fire poorly, often not reaching the necessary temperature, and the kiln could be dangerous. If you're unsure of the power requirements necessary for any of the electrical equipment, seek an electrician's advice. As an extra safety precaution, fit heavy-duty equipment, such as kilns and pug mills, with a safety-approved external cutoff switch to interrupt the electricity at the main electrical box.

The combination of electrical equipment and water presents the risk of electric shock. In accordance with building safety codes, check the proximity of electrical sockets and water taps for safe use. Make sure all electrical appliances are well insulated and maintained, and never use wet hands when touching switches or outlets. Have a qualified electrician fit sealed, waterproof switches to equipment such as wheels and clay mixers that are regularly used in wet conditions.

SPACE

It's a given that if you have a shelf or a cart you'll put something on it. Adequate storage is an important part of organizing a ceramic studio because it frees precious floor space, and clean, uncluttered floors are ideal. It makes sense to place ware carts and shelving close to work areas, bringing boards to them as they fill (you'll get that much-needed stretch, too). Even if you don't move carts often, at least you'll have the option. At a minimum, stow heavy items under your worktables on wooden pallets or low dollies, in case of a water leak. The Lindsay-McLaughlin studio has an under-stair storage area for clay near the studio entrance that makes deliveries easier, and their worktables are just a few steps away.

Storage space is usually at a premium, but shelving expands its capacity.

Use a simple system of organization. Labeling shelves may seem fussy, but such a streamlined approach makes the work that much easier for you, an assistant, or a visiting artist-friend. Plainly put, you'll save time and energy. Shelves near the kiln-loading area are good for posts, firing cones, gloves, and safety goggles. Stand heavier items, such as buckets of kiln wash and kiln shelves, on the floor directly under them.

Shelving units, ware boards, and throwing bats made of sanded and splinter-free wood should be at least 1 inch (2.5 cm) thick to be able to hold the weight of clay and other heavy materials. Apply polyurethane or another water-repellent product to wood shelves so they don't warp when washed. When working with clay chemicals, it's best to rely on metal, plastic-laminate, or other nonporous countertop material.

Sometimes an entire room, rather than an individual kiln, is vented.

EQUIPMENT, ET CETERA

For almost every task in the ceramic studio process, someone has devised a tool that makes it faster and easier. Some ceramic artists find it impossible to work without a favorite piece of equipment, while others design and make whatever they need. Do some comparison shopping before purchasing a major piece of ceramic equipment. If you're on a tight budget, make sure that the slab roller you want is really necessary. Many slab rollers have been turned into ordinary, if expensive, tables because the artist discovered that it was just as simple to use a rolling pin for the occasional slab.

Different styles of equipment influence the final ceramic result in important ways, so ceramists sometimes collect and use a variety of wheels, kilns, and smaller tools. Forms from Cynthia Bringle's electric wheel look different than those thrown on her handmade treadle wheel. Ben Owen has three pug mills: one for porcelain, one for earthenware, and another for stoneware, so there's less contamination of materials. Suze Lindsay has dozens of McLaughlin-made brushes.

Other types of studio equipment, such as extruders, scales, and banding wheels, are also helpful. Mount an extruder, which produces a variety of shapes and hollow forms, securely onto a post or column so you can operate it from many angles and sides. Use other parts of the post to hang extruder accessories, such as dies. A banding wheel lets you turn even fragile pieces as you work on them. Choose a sturdy one that rotates smoothly and precisely, with heavy-duty bearings that will keep the work well balanced.

Materials and tools have aesthetic appeal too.

THE SOURCE OF HEAT

Kilns are one of the most important pieces of equipment in the ceramic studio. Of course you should plan carefully before choosing and installing yours. Since every type of kiln produces results considered unique to that design, think carefully about what you want in the finished ceramic work before purchasing or building a kiln.

Electric Kilns

The electric kiln, which fires work in an oxidizing atmosphere, is easily the most popular kiln type. There are two types of top-load designs, available in a variety of sizes and temperature

Have a gas technician check gas fittings.

or separate room, away from day-to-day studio activities. Even if this isn't an option, you must outfit the kiln with a compatible vent system, powerful enough for the job, that pulls the fumes from the main work area. Strive to create a kiln environment with proper air circulation; ensure that fresh air moves into the studio, and that dust, fumes, and toxins move out. For extra safety, a carbon-monoxide detector is a good idea.

Fuel Kilns

Fuel kilns such as gas, wood, salt, and raku are best suited for protected outdoor sites, preferably away from any buildings. If these kilns are placed too close to the studio, their smoke and noxious fumes can soon find their way inside, creating health and safety risks for inhabitants. Even if your studio is in a rural location, take the time to learn about local regulations for air quality.

GAS

A gas kiln is a versatile tool. Using low or high temperatures, it's possible to produce both oxidizing and reducing atmospheres in them. An outdoor gas kiln must be sheltered in a fireproof structure with fresh air access, completely protected from wind and moisture. Only a nonturbulent environment will give consistent, reliable results. If you install a gas kiln in the studio itself, be sure to position it so that the manufacturer's minimum clearances are met, and use an insulated kiln hood to pull gasses out of the kiln and outdoors. No matter where you install it, get technical support from both the manufacturer and certified gas plumbers. Using the wrong materials for gas hookup and ventilation can have serious consequences.

WOOD, SALT & RAKU KILNS

When used as kiln fuel, wood produces unique and enriching surfaces on ceramic work, but this type of firing involves long hours of intensive physical labor; in fact, it's almost a lifestyle.

Keep high quality seasoned wood in a sheltered space near the kiln.

requirements (up to cone 10). The sectional style, with stacked 9-inch (23 cm) sections, is easier to move or repair than the one-piece design. Electric kilns are well suited to multifired work such as that of figurative ceramic artist Debra Fritts. Although the kiln is inside her studio, she installed proper ventilation to pull the kiln gasses outside, and the walls around the kiln are lined with fireproof panels. Have a licensed electrician help you install your kiln, following the manufacturer's recommendations. Automatic kiln controllers can free you from constant kiln watching during firing, but all manufacturers recommend that you monitor the equipment from the period near the end of the firing through its final shutdown.

A motorized (rather than passive) electric kiln vent is essential to remove the particles, gasses, and toxins that are the by-products of firing clay and glazes in an electric kiln. One of the most dangerous of these is carbon monoxide, which is color-less, odorless, and deadly. Locate the kiln in a well-vented area

Fuel kilns are more complex to operate than are electric ones.

Depending on the size of the kiln and the ceramist's output, the kiln might be fired only a few times each year. Keep high quality, seasoned wood in a sheltered space near the kiln itself. Salt and soda kilns also create specialized effects in a single firing, but they also produce toxic fumes. Take special precautions when adding the salt or soda.

In American raku firing, the glowing-hot work is removed from the kiln with special tongs. The work is then placed in a container holding highly combustible material, such as wood shavings or dry leaves, covered, and left to reduce. Wear goggles, gloves, and a protective apron, and be sure to protect your hair. The process requires little in the way of special equipment, but plenty of careful attention to avoid burns and accidents.

No matter what kind of kiln you use, be sure to make careful, informed decisions about its placement, exhaust ventilation, proper respirators, and even the clothing you wear during firing. Whenever possible have an assistant when firing, in case of an accident or emergency; keep a certified, wall-mounted fire extinguisher in the areas with the greatest potential for fire hazard, as well as a first-aid kit.

Liquid glazes are safer than powdered glaze chemistry.

GLAZE HEALTH

Whether you use a simple sponged-on oxide wash or require multiple airbrushed layers of glazes, glaze chemicals must be handled respectfully. Always use a fitted respirator with the appropriate dust filter, as

Store clay powders in a well-ventilated area.

well as latex gloves, to limit contact with these hazardous powders. Store both raw glaze materials and mixed glazes in airtight, lidded bins or plastic tubs, clearly labeled with the name and recipe. Note whether they're toxic or not, plus any necessary usage instructions or special precautions. In the United States, ceramists may obtain free Material Safety Data Sheets (MSDS) from the manufacturer disclosing the chemicals and compounds used in those glazes. To prevent contamination of materials from bin to bin, use a separate, labeled scoop for each one. Since storage space is often a problem, you might consider storing buckets of glaze on special glazing racks or wheeled carts. Ben Owen keeps quite a few large plastic trash bins full of mixed glaze on wooden tables at a comfortable height for dipping and pouring. His simple, ergonomic approach helps prevent back pain.

Mixing

Wearing a respirator and gloves, mix glazes on a nonporous surface in a well-ventilated area of the studio; keep the necessary tools (gram scales, scoops, sieves) close at hand. Once mixed, most glazes must be sieved several times to ensure a smooth consistency, but don't sieve dry glaze materials, or they'll become airborne. The glazing process can be sloppy, so keep the floor free of unnecessary clutter, and clean spills right away.

Spraying

As with many stages in the ceramic process, spraying poses special hazards for the artist. Spray booth units come in many sizes with various degrees of spraying capacity and ventilation, but a homemade setup works, too, as long as it effectively traps airborne particles. For the protection of your health and that of the environment, outfit the booth with a filtered extractor fan that produces enough suction power for the total cubic area. An alternative design employs a curtain of water at the back of the booth.

Dipping & Brushing

Some glazes work best with a dip application. Use latex gloves or dipping tongs when working with toxic materials, and avoid skin contact. If you apply glazes with a brush, use sturdy ones that won't put loose brush hairs in the glaze bucket.

Organization makes the studio safer and more efficient.

Make the office a dust-free place for slides and paperwork.

THE PAPER DILEMMA

Many artists think of paperwork as a necessary evil (and the studio space they begrudgingly allot to it reflects that reality), yet the office must be a fact of life for the successful, solvent ceramic artist. Keeping slides and images of the work protected and organized makes life much easier in the long run—it's too easy to miss a deadline when you can't find what you need. If you have slides of your work for exhibitions and publications, these must be stored far from clay dust. If you use a computer for your day-to-day billing and studio records, dust can be destructive to electronics, so you'll have to carve out a separate space for the work. On the one hand, if your attitude is "out of sight, out of mind," almost any nook or cubby will do. On the other hand, consider Alice Munn's approach: her serene upper-level office area overlooks the studio, with plenty of windows, space, and art nearby.

A studio gallery space draws visitors.

THE STUDIO GALLERY

Should your studio include a sales gallery? That depends, of course, on whether or not you want visitors. There are monetary advantages to personally handling sales, though marketing concerns and retail traffic steal time from the clay. I recommend some sort of display space, public or private, that will let you revisit your work after it comes from the kiln. The experience can lead you to new ideas and creative progress. The amenities needn't be elaborate or expensive. Properly adjusted track lighting, white walls, and simple, white-painted wooden pedestals you can make yourself seem to enhance most

ceramic pieces' best qualities. For inspiration, consider Mike Vatalaro's elegant display of a few choice pieces in his home's foyer, or build your business as has Ben Owen, who employs a staff member to run his sales gallery and museum in a building separate from the production facilities.

In the next section are profiles of 12 artists in their studios. These exciting work spaces of utility and beauty illustrate dozens of creative studio solutions, and whether the ceramists have small spaces or showcase places, their practical, inventive ways of working may inspire your clay studio.

FIGURATIVE SCULPTOR'S
Space

Debra Fritts' suburban sculpting studio

makes the most of a modest-size room plus

a courtyard with tiled timbers.

iving and working in an Atlanta suburb, Debra Fritts built a creative oasis from what was once a suburban carport. The ceramic studio, attached to a 70s-era house, is an extension of her home. Located on a quiet parcel, the studio sits on a heavily wooded, secluded lot.

Although this is Debra's third studio, it's the first with luxuries such as heat and running hot and cold water, as well as much-needed air conditioning for the hot Georgia summers.

The Fritts studio's courtyard is an extension of the studio. The relief tiles are by Debra, and she displays work by other artists, too.

A vaulted, painted ceiling and lots of windows fill the studio with light and space.

Debra's glaze test forms

Kiln furniture sits neatly under a hand-building table.

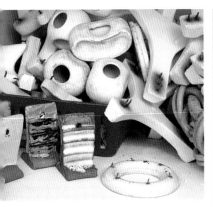

Kiln furniture

Inspiration for the space came from time she spent as a child in a friend's mother's painting studio, and her plans took shape as soon as she bought the home in 2001. Debra's building consultant, a student's husband, solved a problem that would otherwise have slowed the studio's construction process dramatically. Her plywood floor had to be built 12 inches (30.5 cm) above the concrete pad to allow electrical wires and plumbing to lay at the level of the original floor without disturbing it. Within one month of Debra's moving in, the studio's construction was finished.

Texture comes from many sources.

Keeping a visual/verbal journal is an important part of the artist's creative process.

Three pairs of double-hung windows, and French doors at the wood-enclosed courtyard entry, unify the interior space with its delightfully leafy outdoor environment. True to Debra's childhood memory, the studio is just off the kitchen, and she can work there anytime. She fires kilns at night and checks on work in progress throughout the day. The courtyard is an extension of the studio; when the weather is pleasant, Debra creates her hand-built figurative sculptures on the courtyard floor.

Evening draws near.

Cutouts in the fence become display niches for smaller pieces.

Initial construction begins on a worktable; larger pieces will later be moved to a rolling sculptor's stand.

Neat organization and orderly work habits allow Debra to use her small studio space to maximum advantage, and there's enough floor space and openness around the forms for her to effectively appraise her progress. The ceramist first forms a figure on a wheeled sculpture stand. Two worktables serve a variety of needs; on the plaster-topped one, smaller pieces receive their finishing touches. Debra hopes to replace her inexpensive shelving units with built-ins as funds allow. Out-of-the-way nooks display vignettes of found objects (a broken bit of concrete countertop, beach ephemera) whose textures, in time, will become part of her work.

One shelf unit is used for display and glaze storage.

At present, the slab roller is a work surface, since her current pieces are made by pinch-and-coil construction. A pair of electric kilns, one full size and the other a test unit, are located at the back of the studio, where the walls are lined with a fireproof construction board. A heat-recovery vent at the bottom of the kiln removes the expelled gasses, but eventually she will build an enclosed kiln area. Damp-mopping at the end of each working day controls the clay dust.

As a full-time artist, Debra has a routine that necessarily limits weekday distractions. Instead, she hosts an open house twice a year for her ceramics students, and collectors and dealers visit by appointment. She often works (with meal breaks) until 10 p.m. That diligence pays off with regular showings of her finished pieces.

Each morning in this small but infinitely satisfying studio, Debra first reviews her results from yesterday's work, then moves to a small table where she faithfully journals ideas and sketches, and then begins another day.

Debra created a nook where she can sketch and journal.

Heat-resistant board protects the walls and floor of the kiln area.

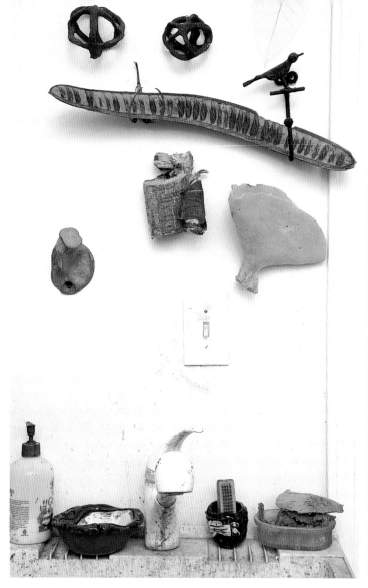

The wall above a studio sink makes a great exhibit space.

Figurative sculptor Debra Fritts in her Roswell, Georgia, studio

ABOUT THE ARTIST

Debra W. Fritts is the director of the ceramics program at the Roswell Arts Center in Roswell, Georgia. She received her undergraduate degree in Art Education from the University of Tennessee, Knoxville, and continued graduate studies in ceramic sculpture and painting at Penland School of Crafts in North Carolina and Arrowmont School of Arts and Crafts in Tennessee. Debra taught art for 13 years in Tennessee, and she has recently conducted master classes and workshops at Georgia State University, Columbus State University, and other southeastern art centers.

Debra enjoys national recognition for her work in ceramic sculpture through invitational exhibitions and awards, gallery representation, private collections, and publications. She has been distinguished as a guest artist and represented by a number of prestigious galleries.

Debra Fritts studio
Roswell, Georgia

This small but hardworking studio is just 300 square feet (27 m²). The artist sculpts in the area with the most natural light, shown by the broken circle on the floor plan. The kiln will eventually be moved out of the studio and into a shed.

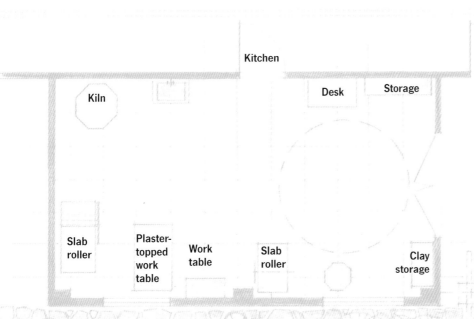

Kitchen

Kiln

Desk **Storage**

Slab roller

Plaster-topped work table

Work table

Slab roller

Clay storage

Debra Fritts

GALLERY

Holding the Circle, 2002. 44 x 15 x 9 in. (110 x 37.5 x 22.5 cm); terra-cotta; hand-built slabs and coils; slips, oxide stains, glazes and underglazes; multiple fired, cone 2 and cone 04. Photo by Michael Noa.

Overflow, 2002. 15 x 11 x 9.5 (37.5 x 27.5 x 23.8 cm); terra-cotta; metal faucet; hand-built coil; slips, glazes and underglazes, oxides; multiple fired, cone 2 and cone 04. Photo by Michael Noa.

The Wait, 2002. 27 x 9 x 5 (67.5 x 22.5 x 12.5 cm); terra-cotta; hand-built coil; slips, glazes and underglazes, oxides; multiple fired, cone 2 and cone 04. Photo by Michael Noa.

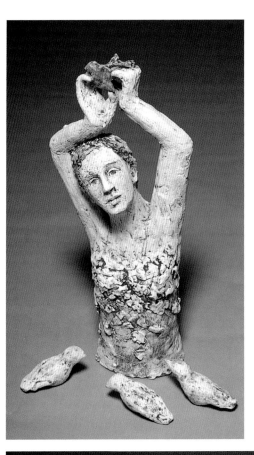

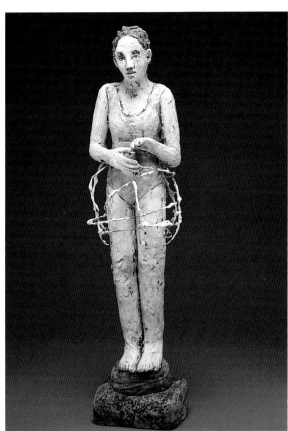

◀ ◀ *Gathering*, 2002.
24 x 19 x 8.5 in. (60 x 47.5 x 21.3 cm); terra-cotta; hand-built coil and slab, modeling; slips, glazes and underglazes, layering oxides; multiple fired, cone 2 and cone 04. Photo by Michael Noa.

◀ *Perfect Fit*, 2001.
24 x 7 x 7 (60 x 17.5 x 17.5 cm); terra-cotta; high temperature wire coated with slip; hand-built coils; slips, stains, glazes, oxides; multiple fired, cone 2 and cone 04. Photo by Michael Noa.

◀ *Echo*, 2002.
13 x 14 x 5 in. (32.5 x 35 x 12.5 cm); terra-cotta; metal funnel; hand-built coil; slips, glaze, underglazes, oxides; multiple fired, cone 2 and cone 04. Photo by Michael Noa.

POTTER'S
Center

Studio potter Ben Owen III built a showcase space designed for maximum efficiency and beauty. The modern layout welcomes thousands of visitors each year.

As you enter the studio, several stages of the pottery process are within view.

The Ben Owen Pottery in Seagrove, North Carolina

Steeped in generations of pottery-making history, Ben Owen III works in a studio surrounded by the rolling farmland of Seagrove, North Carolina. For 250 years, local craftspeople have been producing functional and decorative clay arts there. From this long tradition grew the showcase studio of Ben Owen Pottery, where wheel-thrown production potting continues to flourish.

The two-story studio and its secondary structures stand on property that's been passed from one generation of potters to the next. Ben himself learned how to throw at age eight from Ben Sr. Part of his grandfather's original studio still stands, restored as a museum to display a collection of all of the Owens' work. It also holds ancient Far East clay pots Ben III collected during his travels.

Each of Ben's wheels is positioned so that potter and visitors alike have a view.

The museum features a collection of Owen pottery and historical artifacts, located in the same renovated log cabin as the sales gallery.

Efficient use of the floor, counters, and shelves keeps all materials within easy reach in the glaze-mixing room.

Using a plan that he worked out with a friend who's a local designer, Ben built the studio in 1999. The autoclaved aerated concrete blocks, building materials that are 80 percent air, are one of the many unusual features of the structure. Ben has said that the studio's design is almost like that of a kiln. It's virtually fireproof, and the building materials and paint he used inside it allow him, periodically, to hose down the entire place. All of the floor drains, each with a built-in trap, are connected to a central trap and an environmentally friendly containment area outside.

Spent cones at the site of the wood kiln

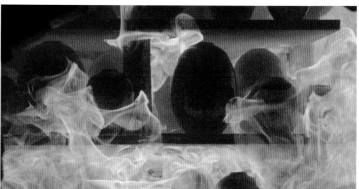

Pots aflame

The spacious sales gallery can handle the busy season's high retail traffic.

Each of the pottery's six electric wheels is dedicated to a single type of clay.

Ben Owen Pottery is a very efficient studio. One of the owner's priorities was to create separate areas for throwing stoneware, porcelain, and earthenware clay, yet relate all the stages of their separate processes to maximize the flow of the work. Ben keeps the gallery supplied with work that collectors and clients have admired for many years, throwing and finishing every piece himself. A full-time employee maintains the kilns, prepares wood, and works on special projects, while another manages the retail gallery and helps with waxing and glazing work. A high school student works four afternoons a week to mix and weigh Ben's clay. Ben often creates a body of work with a theme, such as "Service with Style" or "Tea." His gallery work is popular, and he has many repeat customers who learn of kiln openings by direct mail, through his website, and via email. On the big day it's not unusual to see over 50 people lined up, waiting for the gallery to open. More than 50,000 people—tourists, potters, students, and collectors—visit Ben's gallery and studio every year.

Visitors to the pottery have the opportunity to watch the potter in action.

The pottery's wood-and-glass entry is a striking focal point, and the interior space, with its clean lines, broadly arched doorways, and warm-painted plaster walls, has something of a Mediterranean feel to it. Just inside the doors are three throwing alcoves where visitors can watch Ben work, and ask questions. Saturdays are especially busy, when as many as 100 or more people might pass through the studio. Many take advantage of the wheel area's rocking chairs and the welcoming fire in the fireplace. Helpful signs identify the purpose of each work area so visitors are free to do a self-tour. There's a full-size kitchen for staff and, upstairs, a large living room, guest room, weight room, and bath.

Ben's basic throwing tools

The next room in the studio houses three pug mills (one for each clay type), which remove air from the clay and ready it for throwing. The adjacent area holds ware carts and large tubs of Ben's high-fire glazes. In yet another room, three electric kilns bisque the green ware, and there's also a ventilated area for waxing pot bottoms. In a particularly dramatic-looking room, Ben applies his signature red glaze on earthenware pots before they go to the electric kilns dedicated solely to firing them. It's a toxic glaze, so the artist must take care to isolate these materials and processes from all others.

Separate pug mills ensure that none of the clay bodies is contaminated by foreign clay.

Procedures associated with the distinctive but toxic Chinese-red glaze for which Ben is known must be kept separate from all other processes, materials, and equipment.

Ben typically starts work early—with coffee—and builds a fire if the studio is chilly. He spends his mornings throwing or trimming work from the day before. Some afternoons are spent glazing work for the electric or wood kiln. Ben must work for two to three weeks in a constant rhythm of throwing, trimming, and glazing in order to fill one of his single-chamber wood kilns. These are in a large covered kiln area adjacent to the 4,000-square-foot (360 m²) studio. In addition to the salt kiln, a new anagama kiln stands next to the one Ben's grandfather built decades earlier. A building that holds clay-mixing equipment and raw ceramic material resides near the kiln yard.

In a holding room, ware carts hold work that is ready to move to or from the kiln shed.

The kiln compound contains many kilns, including anagama, groundhog, gas- and wood-fired, and catenary designs.

A porch swing makes long hours of firing a little more pleasant.

Ben worked for a time at the International Workshop of Ceramic Art (IWCA) in Tokoname, Japan. "Japanese studio design inspired me to build one of my own where I could spend more time being creative and less time just moving things around," he says. The studio's unique waterfall spray booth is a copy of one at the IWCA's Shigaraki Ceramic Culture Park. Water flows down the stainless steel wall and into a holding pool at its base; the booth's strong ventilation system captures any glaze that escapes the water. It's interesting that the exposure to Eastern methods and style influenced both Ben and Ben Sr.

Inspiration for this waterfall-style spray booth came from a similar one Ben used in Japan.

Many visitors to his pottery ask Ben what it takes to be a potter and run a studio. In the spirit of his pioneering potter ancestors, and with a lifetime of throwing under his belt, Ben's answer comes quickly: "First you learn to make pots. Then you should learn to be a brick mason, an electrician, a plumber, and a chemist. The more you can do, the better things will go."

ABOUT THE ARTIST

Ben Owen III is a traditional potter from Seagrove, North Carolina. He learned to make pottery from his grandfather, Ben Owen, Sr., and earned his B.F.A. in ceramics from East Carolina University. He owns and operates Ben Owen Pottery, one of the more than 100 area potteries.

Ben exhibits his work extensively throughout the U.S. He also teaches workshops in pottery making and kiln building. His works can be found in many private collections as well as museum collections. Articles and reviews of Ben's work have appeared in various publications, including Smithsonian Magazine, The New York Times, and Studio Potter and Clay Times magazines.

Ben Owen III Pottery
Seagrove, North Carolina

All six throwing wheels are located in a wide, welcoming foyer that can hold many visitors
at any given time. A chain of special-purpose rooms lead to the gas and wood kilns,
and a loading dock abuts the gas kiln area.

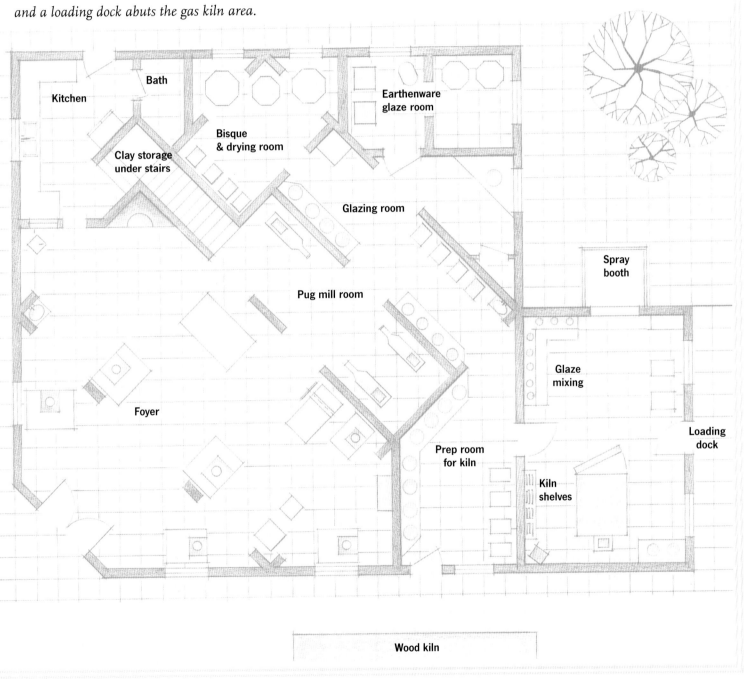

Kitchen

Bath

Clay storage
under stairs

Bisque
& drying room

Earthenware
glaze room

Glazing room

Spray
booth

Pug mill room

Glaze
mixing

Foyer

Loading
dock

Prep room
for kiln

Kiln
shelves

Wood kiln

Ben Owen
GALLERY

▶ *Tang Vases*, 1997.
6 x 9 x 12 in. (15 x 22.5 x 30
cm); stoneware; Chinese blue
glaze; wood kiln, cone 9.
Photo by David H. Ramsey.

▲ *Sea Biscuit*, 2002. 15 x 15 x 5 in. (37.5 x 37.5 x 12.5 cm); stoneware;
salt glaze; wood kiln, cone 10. Photo by David H. Ramsey.

◀ *Bottle*, 2001. 26 in. (65 cm);
porcelain; ash glaze; wood kiln,
cone 11. Photo by David H. Ramsey.

Covered Jar, 2002.
24 x 14 x 14 in. (60 x 35 x 35 cm);
stoneware; Oribe glaze; wood kiln,
cone 11. Photo by David H. Ramsey.

Carved Bowls, 2001. 5 x 8 x 11 in.
(12.5 x 20 x 27.5 cm); stoneware; copper glaze;
wood kiln, cone 10. Photo by David H. Ramsey.

Bottle, 2001, 33 in. (82.5 cm); earthenware;
Chinese red glaze; low fire kiln, cone 07, Photo by David H. Ramsey

TWO POTTERS'
Studio

Kent McLaughlin and Suze Lindsay make thrown-and-altered

vessels in a spacious structure even as they plan

to further refine the remote but increasingly

popular mountainside pottery.

View from Fork Mountain Road. All the studio's large windows are facing the woods.

The husband-and-wife potter team of Suze Lindsay and Kent McLaughlin shares a spacious, light, and airy studio on Fork Mountain near the Tennessee–North Carolina border. Their home and studio, situated above a forested valley, are companionably close—near enough to each other so that the couple is never far from their life's interests: pot making, the vegetable garden, and their pets.

Kent and Suze's decision to build their studio in this area grew out of their experiences of working at the nearby Penland School of Crafts. It was also helpful to know some artisan-friends who were already established in the area. Their move, inspired by their growing love for the wild mountainous region, was a natural one and a good fit.

The two ceramists gave careful thought to the cyclical flow of a studio pottery. They collaborated on the initial design, yet the space has, from its beginning in 1995, contained the seeds of their shared vision for its future. Kent, Suze, and

Every workstation has a view.

Kent's slip bowl

friends completed the majority of the wood-frame building's construction within a three-year period. Looking to the day when they might need a resident assistant for heavier work, they included a loft, which presently serves as office, guest room, and Kent's place to create his handmade brushes. During the initial building phase, an existing 14 x 18-foot (4.2 x 5.4 m) cinderblock shed served as the pottery—a tight fit. It's now the glaze-mixing house and provides out-of-the-way storage for bulky raw materials.

Both artists create thrown functional and decorative pottery; Suze single-fires in the salt kiln that Kent helped her build, and Kent fires in a cone-10 commercial reduction kiln. Suze only uses a treadle, but Kent moves between wheels of different designs. Each wheel has a view into the woods. When the two artists first started making work at their Fork Mountain Pottery, they had no kiln. With dry, decorated greenware on her lap, Suze drove the winding narrow roads to a friend's salt kiln 6 miles (9.6 km) away.

Metal brackets affixed to the wheels' wooden frames hold a ware board. When it's full of work, the shelf is moved to a wheeled cart. Rolling carts work well in this 1800-square-foot (600 m²) space, saving the ceramists a lot of steps. Several sawhorse tables and plenty of floor space allow them to create larger work, too. Even with so much room, the slab roller in front of Suze's worktable often multi-tasks as an extra work surface, especially for press molding. Full carts, ready for the kilns, wait near the door that opens onto the kiln pad. Kent bisques his work before glazing it at a broad table. Suze first decorates and glazes her greenware; it takes three carts' work to fill her salt kiln.

Along the back of the kiln shed and studio is a cantilevered wooden deck.

Kent moves between several styles of wheels.

Tools and inspiration at Kent's worktable

Work moves through the studio on a six-week cycle. In the morning, Suze begins at the wheel, or trims and adds handles to work she made the day before. Kent likes to make handmade brushes for a couple of hours before getting his hands in the clay. When work is in full swing, they usually get 10 to 12 hours a day in the studio. Both artists are often busy with travel to workshops and conferences, too, so time in the studio is precious.

The studio has excellent cross ventilation. In the warmer months its ceiling fans circulate the cool air that flows up the mountainside from the woods, keeping the room comfortable without air conditioning. The studio is heated with a gas heater and a wood stove. Kent lined the corner around the wood stove with fire-retardant boards mounted 2 inches (5.1 cm) away from the walls and floor. The airspace lets the heat move freely through the studio rather than trapping it in the wall.

Inspiration for Suze's slightly modified vessels comes from found natural objects. In summertime her garden is full of flowers and butterflies.

A few of Suze's tools at her worktable, which is snuggled up to a multi-tasking slab roller.

Kent's slightly modified chair

Several years ago Suze, Kent, and 12 other local clay artists formed a loose cooperative known as Potters of the Roan. They worked together to design a logo and identical wooden signposts, a website, and a glossy brochure, which help visitors find these lonesome rural potteries, especially during their big biannual open houses and studio tours. When construction first started on the main studio, Kent built a small barnlike structure to store building materials. They now use this warm, rustic space, which is the one nearest the road, as their sales and gallery area. During daylight hours, its barn doors stand open, rain or shine. As with most craft shops in this area, visitors can handle their own smaller sales transactions with an informal honor system (money in a tin box) if the proprietors are busy.

Both Suze and Kent are strong believers in using preventive measures to save their backs and legs. Foam floor pads serve as antifatigue mats wherever the artists stand to work. The painted floors, made from full sheets of 1-inch (2.5 cm) shock-absorbing plywood, also provide a cushioned surface to walk on. Kent modified a worn wooden café chair he uses at his low electric wheel. He shortened its front legs, which allows him to lean forward more naturally, with less back strain. Suze uses an ergonomic "kneeling stool" at her glazing table.

Suze's work area is furnished with memorabilia, a painted wood floor, and a great view.

The sign above the gallery proclaims its wares. This shed held building materials during the studio's three-year construction period.

Suze's salt kiln is just a few steps from the studio.

The glaze house sits next to the kiln pad.

The cathedral ceiling captures all the light in this mountaintop studio.

A post plays a supporting role as tool rack at Kent's electric wheel, eliminating the need for yet another table.

The continued growth of their studio confirms Kent and Suze's enthusiasm for visionary planning; they consider the space to be a work in progress. They recently broke ground for a gallery addition, storage area, and bath, which will add another 640 square feet (192 m²) to the original structure. They'll build Kent's new reduction kiln on the concrete pad extension he poured a couple of summers ago. With one foot firmly in the present and an eye cast toward the future, these artists are continually working to create their ideal of the marriage of artistry and utility.

Clay storage under the loft stairs

Brush-making desk in the guest loft.

Kent and Suze plan to add a large foyer, gallery, and bath to the studio. Foot traffic has increased each year since they joined a potter's cooperative.

Construction on Kent's new gas kiln begins soon.

Kent McLaughlin and Suze Lindsay outside the Fork Mountain Pottery

ABOUT THE ARTISTS

Kent McLaughlin is a studio potter working in western North Carolina. He apprenticed with a production potter for three years in the late 1970s before opening his own studio.

Throughout his career, he has pursued growth and knowledge by attending and assisting in clay workshops at Penland School of Crafts in North Carolina, Haystack Mountain School of Crafts in Maine, and Arrowmont School of Arts and Crafts in Tennessee. A member of the Southern Highland Craft Guild, he has taught, lectured, and demonstrated at Anderson Ranch Arts Center in Colorado, John C. Campbell Folk School and Odyssey Center for the Ceramic Arts in North Carolina, and Brevard Community College in Florida. He exhibits nationally.

Suze Lindsay received her master of fine arts degree from Louisiana State University in 1992, after completing a two-year fellowship study at Penland School of Crafts in western North Carolina. After three years as a resident artist at Penland, she settled in the area, where she and her husband, Kent McLaughlin, own and operate Fork Mountain Pottery.

Suze has taught workshops at numerous art centers and universities, including Arrowmont School of Arts and Crafts in Tennessee, Haystack Mountain School of Crafts in Maine, Ohio University, and Tulane University. Her work is in the permanent collections of The Ohr-O'Keefe Museum of Art in Mississippi, the Islip Art Museum in New York, and the Kennedy Museum of Art in Ohio.

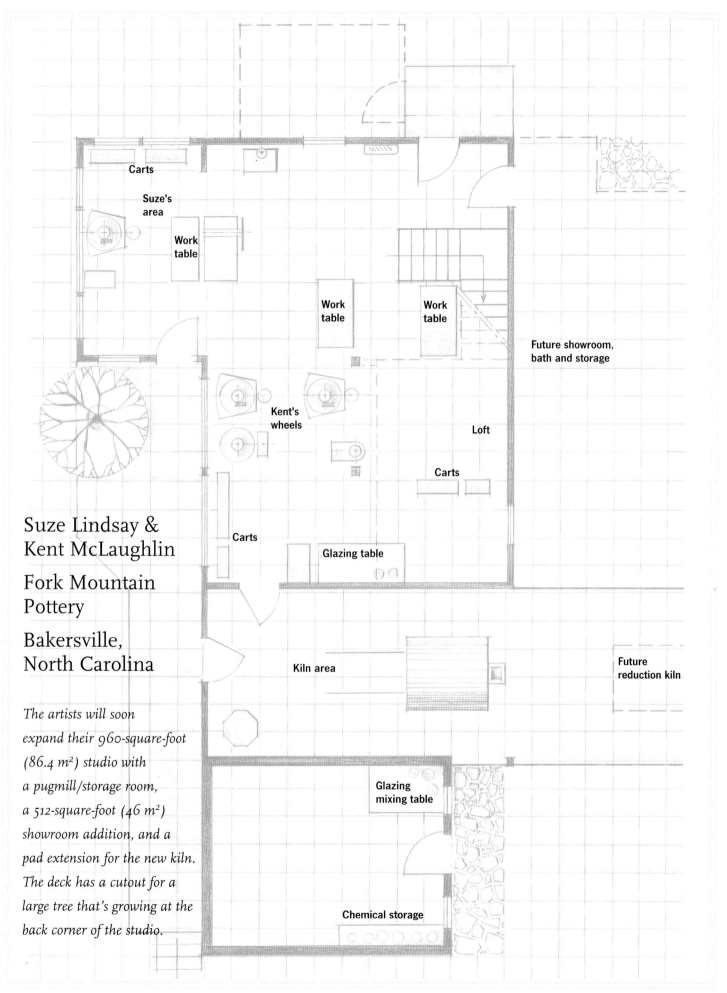

Carts

Suze's area

Work table

Work table

Work table

Future showroom, bath and storage

Kent's wheels

Loft

Carts

Carts

Glazing table

Suze Lindsay & Kent McLaughlin

Fork Mountain Pottery

Bakersville, North Carolina

Kiln area

Future reduction kiln

The artists will soon
expand their 960-square-foot
(86.4 m²) studio with
a pugmill/storage room,
a 512-square-foot (46 m²)
showroom addition, and a
pad extension for the new kiln.
The deck has a cutout for a
large tree that's growing at the
back corner of the studio.

Glazing mixing table

Chemical storage

GALLERY

▲ Suze Lindsay, *Serving Bowls*, 2002. 8 x 9 x 9 in. (20 x 22.5 x 22.5 cm); stoneware; wheel thrown; salt fired, cone 10. Photo by Tom Mills.

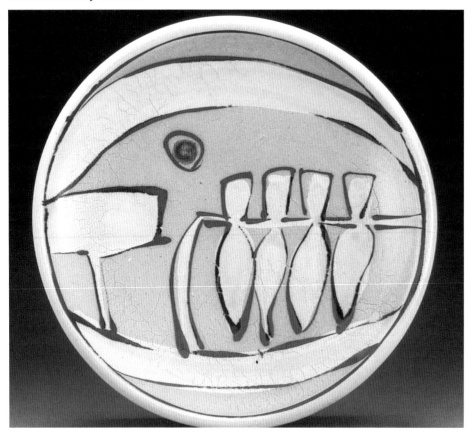

▲ Suze Lindsay, *Platter*, 2002. 2 x 12 x 12 in. (5 x 30 x 30 cm); stoneware; wheel thrown; soda fired, cone 10. Photo by Tom Mills.

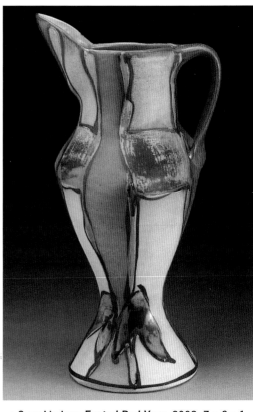

▲ Suze Lindsay, *Footed Bud Vase*, 2002. 7 x 6 x 1 in. (17.5 x 15 x 2.5 cm); stoneware; assembled, thrown, and hand-built elements; salt fired, cone 10. Photo by Tom Mills.

⌃ Kent McLaughlin, *Teapot*, 2002. 4.3 x 4 in. (10.8 x 10 cm); porcelain; wheel thrown and altered; carbon trap shino glaze; cone 10. Photo by Tom Mills.

⌃ Kent McLaughlin, *Rope-Patterned Bowl*, 2002. 5.5 x 16 in. (13.8 x 40 cm); white stoneware; mashiko glaze over celadon glaze; cone 10. Photo by Tom Mills.

⌃ Kent McLaughlin, *Altered Bowls*, 2002. 1.5 x 4 x 6 in. (3.8 x 10 x 15 cm); porcelain; wheel-thrown and altered rim; carbon trap shino glaze; cone 10. Photo by Tom Mills.

The Gray studio overlooks the garden beds. A standing-seam roof unifies the added shed with the original building.

HAND BUILDER'S
Cottage

Figurative clay artist Becky Gray gave her cottage-style converted structure a graceful update with antique windows.

Becky Gray's studio is a truly magical place. It's situated on five wooded acres in western North Carolina, within perhaps the country's oldest land trust and intentional community. Her small cottage sits in a wide green meadow bound by a trout-filled mountain stream and laced with frequent mists. More than 75 years old, this sawdust-and-cement-stuccoed building had first served as a Quaker meetinghouse. Becky obtained permission, in 1975, to use the empty building as a studio.

A salvaged church window graces the semi-enclosed kiln shed. Raku reduction also takes place here.

The studio's original footprint remains. And the fact is that Becky doesn't care to make any exterior changes; the studio is beautiful as it is. Working within their community's guidelines, Becky and her husband were able to transform a dirt-floored storage barn into a functional, well-lit studio with an added-on kiln shed.

Wall space above and around equipment is always put to good use. Here, ware boards sit above the slab roller.

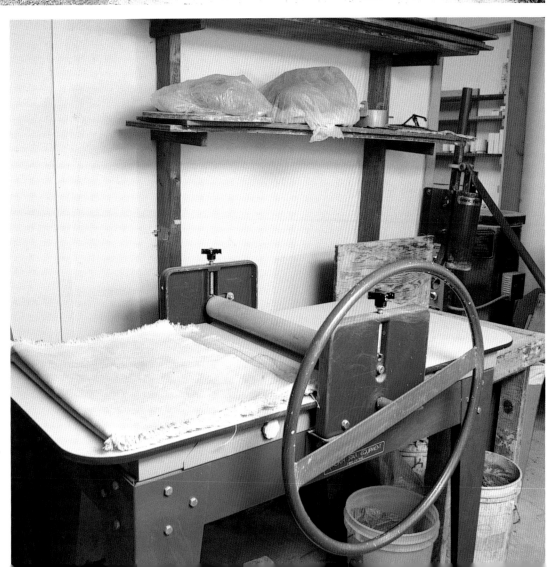

Becky Gray's hand-building studio floor has a drain for easy cleanup.

Remarkable antique windows, salvaged from historic structures, provide some of the studio's natural light and passive solar heat. On sunny afternoons, light pours through a grand old wood-frame window set into the southern wall. Fluorescent ceiling lights are used for night work if the artist has a deadline. She enjoys walking down the hill to her studio, even in the middle of a wakeful night. A propane-fueled raku kiln and sawdust barrels reside under the broad shed roof that extends from the back of the studio proper. The building has no running water, but a stream just outside it gives Becky all she needs.

Birds and brushes are always at hand.

This spare, neat art space has well-worn work surfaces and clay's cool feel, even in summer. The artist organized the area very efficiently, making good use of every speck of space in this 440-square-foot (39.6 m²) building. The L-shaped main room, with a back door that opens onto the kiln shed, holds a central table where the artist does most of her hand building. An alcove gallery, part of the main room, displays her work on a few pedestals, shelves, and a low chest. Countertops wrap one corner, where slab work and thrown elements await assembly on the central worktable. Shelves under the counters provide ample storage for bagged clay, canvas, and tools. Economy of space dictates wall racks with adjustable shelves, rather than ware carts, to hold her greenware and bisque. As with many rural potters' studios, this small space uses a combination of electric and wood-stove heat.

Even small juts in walls are put to good use. Green ware dries on shelves near the woodstove.

The traveling exhibit display is stored in the attic, and some built-in shelves display favorite pieces of work by Becky and other artists. Although she doesn't have many daily visitors, she participates in the area's 100-studio tour for two days in the spring and another two days before the Christmas holidays, when hundreds of people come to buy work.

In the front of the studio, in only half the space of the main room, is the glaze-mixing table, a slab roller, a wedging board, an extruder—there's even room for packing material. Straddling the low opening between the rooms are two different-size kilns that can fire and cool pieces at rates appropriate for the size of the work. Tucked into a windowed corner, with a view of a quiet country road, is her kick wheel. Everything fits the space as if it were meant to be there.

Tucked into an alcove, the wood-floored gallery uses modular units to build the display surfaces.

No space is wasted in the long, narrow front room. A canvas-covered worktable waits by the extruder.

Becky's kick wheel, tucked between the electric kiln and glaze table, overlooks a quiet country road.

Antique windows reference the studio's former life as a Quaker meetinghouse.

Bisque ware goes straight from the kiln to built-in shelves.

A large commission takes shape in the central work space.

Just as Becky and her family are nestled into community life, its work and pleasure marked in seasonal changes, so too have artist, studio, and process become one. She says, "My studio is small, so the work area becomes the glazing area, then the packing area, as I proceed through each phase of the cycle of completing a body of work, and I like this rhythm very much."

ABOUT THE ARTIST

Becky Gray lives in Celo, North Carolina, a land trust and planned community. She received bachelor degrees in English and art from Meredith College in North Carolina, and also attended advanced classes at several other institutions of higher learning in the southeastern United States. Her figurative work has appeared in a large number of group exhibitions as well as a dozen one- and two-person shows. She advises two regional crafts associations and holds membership in the American Crafts Council, the North Carolina Arts Council, and several others. Becky teaches workshops and her work is held in private and public collections, and she was a contributing artist to *Handbuilt Ceramics* (Kathy Triplett; Lark Books, 2000).

Becky Gray at work in the main room, with a small reference library tucked into a corner. Her three excitable terriers couldn't hold still for a portrait.

Becky Gray studio
Celo, North Carolina

The artist makes the most of her 462 square feet (41.5 m²). The central work table is perhaps the most versatile piece of furniture, serving many functions through the various stages of the ceramic process.

Garden

Packing materials

Gallery

Kiln shed

Storage

Counter

Extruder

Work table

Wheel

Kiln area

Sawdust pile

Counter and storage

A view to the bird feeder

Becky Gray
GALLERY

▶ *Persephone*, 1998.
22 x 15 x 12 in. (55 x 37.5 x 30
cm); stoneware; slumped slab
construction; stains and underglazes; raku fired, cone 04.
Photo by John Littleton.

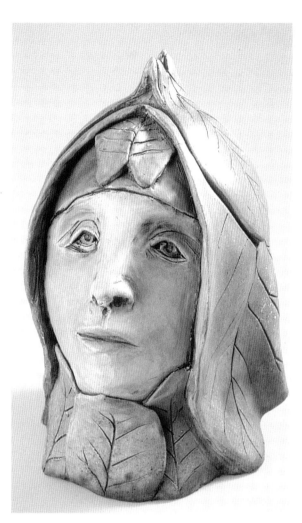

◄ ◄ **Fall Tower,** 1997.
22 x 10 x 10 in. (55 x 25 x 25 cm);
stoneware; altered slab construction; terra sigillata with stain and underglaze; raku fired, cone 04.
Photo by Tim Barnwell.

◄ **Reliquary with Leaves**, 2000.
12 x 6 x 8 in. (30 x 15 x 20 cm);
stoneware; wheel thrown and altered; terra sigillata with stains; raku fired, cone 04.
Photo by John Littleton.

◄ ◄ Becky Gray, **Mother & Daughter,**
2001, 18 x 10 x 8 in. (45 x 25 x 20 cm); stoneware; slumped slab construction with hand-built additions; terra sigillata with stains and underglazes; cone 04 oxidation
Photo by Tom Mills

◄ **Mirror with Guardians**, 2003
42 x 36 in. (3.2 x .9 m); raku-fired stoneware. Photo by Tom Mills.

PRODUCTION POTTERS'
Workshop

A resourceful blend of traditional and modern practice, the Jugtown Pottery, owned by Vern and Pam Owens, has housed several generations of potters.

Traditional wheel-thrown pitchers, bowls, platters, and, yes, jugs rule at the historically rich and scenic Jugtown Pottery, in Seagrove, North Carolina. Respect and appreciation for the past are everywhere in evidence. At this 80-year-old establishment, the roots of modern potters' studios show that methods and forms have changed only slowly. This is where Pam and Vernon Owens make their work.

Ceramics and weaving make natural companions in the sales gallery. Most of the original building's log construction is still in evidence.

Vern's ancestors had clay under their nails, and his own life in clay has been recognized as a national treasure. The history of Seagrove, and that of the Owens family, parallels ceramics' evolution as both useful artifacts and valued cultural and artistic objects. Many of the pottery's log cabins, made from southern pines felled on the property, were built by the community's residents in the 1920s. The couple throws their wares in a cozy two-room cabin. It was only in the mid-1990s that Pam and Vern added insulation, installed more windows, and painted the ceiling white; much remains in this building just as it has always been. The original floors, made of natural earth, are easy on hardworking potters' bodies.

Jugtown Pottery, in Seagrove, North Carolina, is a group of old and new buildings.

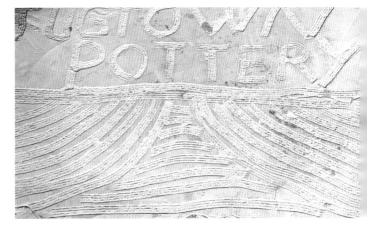

The throwing room is a time capsule of the pottery's history.

Gas car kiln blasting away at the Jugtown Pottery

Jugtown pots are stamped with "Jugtown Ware," the year of their creation, and the initials of the potter. The logo design has been in use since 1921.

An antique double-beam scale at the wedging table

Work is carried on wooden boards from the throwing studio down a small hill to the finishing and drying rooms. Pam enjoys transporting the fresh-made pots because the walk relieves the rigors of the wheel. In the drying room each piece is stamped with the Jugtown emblem (designed at its inception, in 1921) and signed by its maker. The room is kept warm for drying with oil and wood heaters, and a fan circulates the air. This room will be filled with several hundred pots as the work moves through the pottery's eight-day production cycle. The car kiln used for bisque firing is ingeniously located just outside the building, and its tracks extend directly into the finishing room so that it can be loaded regardless of the weather.

The Owenses throw more than 10,000 pots each year.

This groundhog kiln, one of three on the property, is 50 years old.

With such a high production rate, the pieces are necessarily part of an extremely efficient work flow. Bisqued work is waxed and glazed in an updated room that has fluorescent light fixtures and a smooth cement floor. Large batches of glazes are kept in lidded and wheeled plastic buckets. Jugtown's many kilns include two gas car kilns, two groundhog salt kilns (each with 100 cubic feet of stacking space), a large 250-cubic-foot adapted groundhog kiln, and two much smaller kilns: a fast-fire wood kiln and yet another groundhog kiln. Finished work goes either to the packing and shipping room or straight to the retail sales cabin, which attracts many visitors every day—sometimes by the busload.

Many Seagrove generations have dug their local clay, and Pam and Vern's operation upholds this labor-intensive tradition. During warm weather they mix large batches of the local goods with dry clay powder in a protected outdoor area near the drying rooms. The clay is left to age in order to increase its plasticity. A tractor pulls the clay-loaded trailers to the pug mills, which are near the throwing studio.

On a typical day Pam and Vern move yesterday's pots to the drying room to be stamped and cleaned, while leather-hard ones may be trimmed and given handles. Pam and Vern average four hours of throwing each day: two in the morning and two in the after-noon. Mondays are their best workdays, when Jugtown is closed to the public. Naturally, such an operation requires many helping hands.

The Owenses employ four part-time people who work in the office, pack and ship, make clay, or help out in the sales gallery. One full-time worker handles the glazing.

The couple's two school-aged children, Travis and Bailey, are following in their parents' footsteps, throwing and hand building pieces in the old tradition.

Through the decades at Jugtown, much has changed, but the original spirit remains. Hot water and electricity have been added. Lead-based glazes were reformulated, and tractors, rather than horses, move heavy loads. At every turn, the Owenses live with an amazing wealth of ceramic history that is fused into the cracks and corners of the Jugtown Pottery.

Wood stoves are very popular with potters. Notice that the car kiln rails behind it extend well into the studio.

This efficiently placed car kiln can be loaded inside the building.

A newer throwing room shares a wall with one from the original log cabin.

The renovated museum and gallery effortlessly blend old and new.

ABOUT THE ARTISTS

Vern Owens has always lived in Seagrove, North Carolina. He grew up in his father's workshop down the street from the pottery, learning at an early age to throw traditional pots on a treadle wheel.

Vern has received a number of awards that recognize his lifetime contribution to ceramic folk tradition, including a North Carolina Folk Heritage Award from the NC Arts Council in 1994; the National Heritage Fellowship from the National Endowment for the Arts (1996); and an Honorary

Jugtown Pottery owners Pam and Vern Owens stand on either side of son Ben Owens.

Doctor of Humane Letters from North Carolina State University (2000). Vernon collaborated with artist William Mangum in 2000 on the Carolina Preserves Community Arts Project.

As part of her seven-year potter's apprenticeship, Pam Owens first came to the Jugtown Pottery from New Hampshire in the late 1970s. She was drawn by the area's hundreds-years-old pottery tradition, and never left.

Vernon and Pam Owens
Jugtown Pottery
Seagrove,
North Carolina

The pottery's operations take place in a cluster of smaller buildings that stand on either side of the drive that winds through the property. The workshops are separate from the sales gallery and museum, and the pottery's kilns hug the workshop areas.

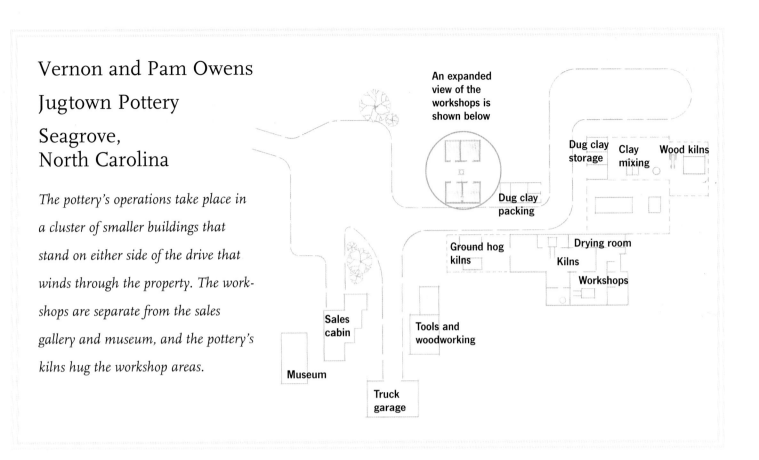

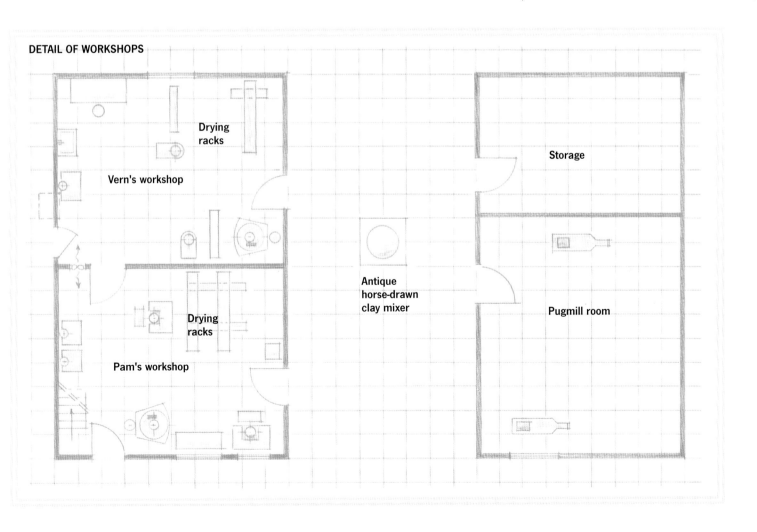

DETAIL OF WORKSHOPS

GALLERY

▲ Pam & Vernon Owens, *Teapot*, 2000. 6 in. (15 cm); stoneware; frog-skin and salt glazes; wood fired in groundhog kiln, cone 10. Photo by Juan Villa.

▲ Pam & Vernon Owens, *Rope Pattern Jar*, 2002. 18 in. (45 cm); stoneware; peach bloom and oxblood glazes; gas reduction in car kiln, cone 10. Photo by Juan Villa.

▲ Pam Owens, *Vase*, 1996. 8 in. (20 cm); red stoneware; copper glaze; wood fired in fast fire kiln, cone 6. Photo by Juan Villa.

▲ Pam Owens, *Jug*, 2001. 9 in. (22.5 cm); stoneware; ash glaze; wood fired in groundhog kiln, cone 10. Photo by Juan Villa.

▲ Vernon Owens, *Vase*, 1991. 13 in. (33 cm) tall; stoneware; Copper Red and salt glazes; wood-fired in groundhog kiln, cone 10. Photo by Juan Villa.

▲ Vernon Owens, *Handled Jar*, 2000. 10 in. (25 cm); salted earthenware clay; copper glaze; wood fired in groundhog kiln, cone 5. Photo by Juan Villa.

HAND BUILDER'S
Atelier

This calm, light-filled studio, an extention
of Alice Munn's home, has fascinating interior
and exterior views in all directions.

Alice Munn's work in clay evokes the beauty and harmony that she finds in the natural world. Her studio, too, is a graceful, balanced space, every corner filled with light and the stones, branches, and feathers that she brings back from her walks and her travels. Large windows in the cathedral-ceiling space face Alice's garden so she can link its rhythms with those of her craft. Living plants add to her inspiration from nature, and windowsills and walls hold changing vignettes of leaves, shells, and seeds. Her studio is very much a self-portrait.

For the past several years Alice and her husband, Roger (an architect and also an artist), have been transforming an older ranch-style home in Greenville, South Carolina, into a spacious, contemporary one that allows plenty of room for both her and Roger's work spaces. As a teacher at two schools, and with an active exhibition schedule, Alice needs a studio connected to her home so she can leave developing projects out on the table, working on them as time allows. The constant presence of Alice's work maintains her connection with her creative process and fulfills her practical needs. She says, "I can wander into it at any time of the day or night. Its convenient location lets me do small tasks in the studio even when I'm cooking, since the kitchen is the next room over from it." Thanks to two outside entrances, Alice can move work and materials without having to go through the house. Protected by the house's eaves, she can airbrush or do sanding on an outdoor table almost anytime in the mild climate, and thus avoids creating dust in the studio.

An eave over the exterior door protects the spray table.

Much of Alice's inspiration comes from the natural world. Her garden is just outside the studio.

As she planned this space, Alice used her experience with her previous three studios as a springboard for ideas about what she wanted. She was aware that she needed light as much as she needed the space for tools and materials. After years of standing on concrete floors (and dealing with the resulting back and foot problems), she was sure she wanted wood flooring and thick rubber padding around the primary worktables. Her years of teaching younger students taught her the essentials of economy and organization, and as a result her working methods are tight and very clean—almost waste-free. The artist uses multitasking tables for drying work, drawing, rolling out seamless paper for photography, and other miscellaneous jobs. One deep built-in alcove stores clay minutia, and another acts as a miniature gallery for some of her favorite pieces. There's a sitting area nearby, complete with a large comfortable chair for relaxing, reading, and sketching. The walls hold photos, drawings, and the ephemera that inspire her work in clay.

Alice moves the airbrush compressor outdoors to apply terra sigillata to a finished form, and she keeps her clay stash small.

A slab roller can often double as an extra worktable.

Shelves in deep, space-efficient alcoves keep materials readily accessible.

A small sitting area for the occasional guest

Glaze tests

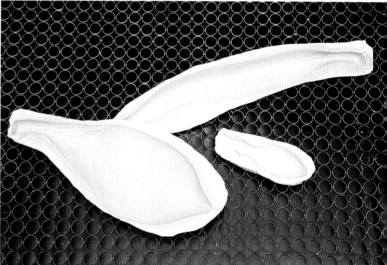
Alice occasionally makes plaster molds; the ultra-thin vinyl flooring came from a super-discount store.

This air-circulating unit traps very fine particles but doesn't require any outside venting, so the studio can stay open to the rest of the house.

The worktable, accessible on all sides, is surrounded by windows. A small slab roller also stores tools. The studio remains open to the rest of the house because a powerful air-cleaning unit, which stands just 12 inches (.3 m) from the worktable, keeps the place dust-free. Once a piece is dry, Alice moves it to the outdoor table for airbrushed applications of terra sigillata; even though she's outside, she wears a protective mask. Since the table is under the eaves, she isn't particularly limited by weather conditions. Her burnishing tools are simple: she favors plastic grocery bags or soft nylon hosiery. Alice's electric kiln is stored in her husband's woodworking studio until they complete their next stage of studio refinement, adding a separate building. Until then, Alice fires her work at school; there she also stores and displays her work. The institution allows her to draw from its great supply of sturdy computer boxes, foams, and storage space, thus solving problems that many clay artists struggle with.

Sources, test tiles, bisque ware, and glaze piece: the main worktable holds several stages of the hand-building process at once.

True to the philosophy that less is more, Alice's production level is deliberately low, and she doesn't need to keep a lot of clay on hand. A bag of white earthenware sits on the floor next to a pair of tables while she hand builds, but goes back under the sink once she's finished. This moderate use of materials suits her small space. And yet, when she has an upcoming exhibit, she can step up her pace and put on a large show without difficulty. For large-scale pieces, she creates forms from smaller components.

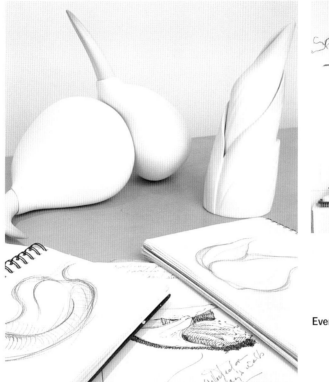

Every task area is neat.

Clean white space is essential to this artist's process.

The orderly office has multiple views of the studio and the outdoors, and there's even a glass section in the floor over the kitchen.

Windows in the overhead office let Alice stay visually connected to several indoor and outdoor areas.

The airy studio, made of wood, glass, and light, is simply an extension of the house; Alice Munn's pieces and her working method—even the structure itself—reflect and influence each other in a flow of philosophy and practice.

Grouping tools in similar containers adds to the sense of order and calm.

Alice Munn in her one-room studio in Greenville, South Carolina

Alice Munn studio
Greenville, South Carolina

The layout of this 540-square-foot (48.6 m²) studio is consistent with an aesthetic of pared-down utility. The office overhead is connected to the studio and to nature by the many windows that pierce walls and floor.

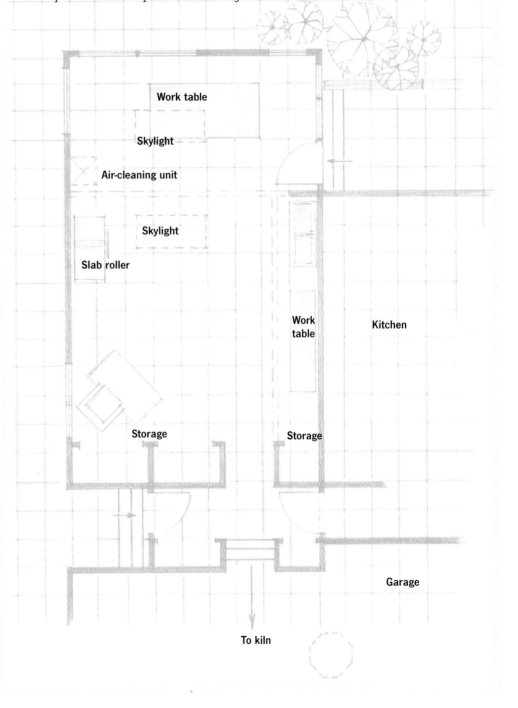

ABOUT THE ARTIST

Alice Ballard Munn teaches ceramics at the Governor's School for the Arts and Humanities in Greenville, South Carolina; she also teaches art at the Christ Church Episcopal School in the same city. She received both a B.S. and her M.F.A. from the University of Michigan.

Although trained as a painter, Alice has had a passion for making ceramic sculpture for 30 years. She exhibits primarily in the southeastern United States, but her participation in shows around the country has garnered recognition at the national level. Her work is in the permanent collection of the Smithsonian American Art Museum's Renwick Gallery in Washington, and is represented in several books on ceramics.

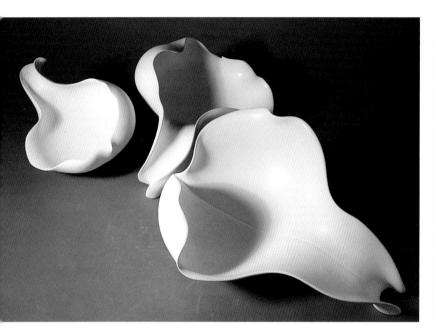

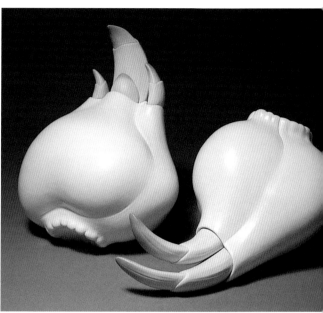

▲ *Evolution of a Garden*, 2001. 6 x 18 x 14 in. (15 x 45 x 35 cm); white earthen-ware; slab and pinch; brushed terra sigillata; cone 06. Photo by artist.

▲ *Narcissus Pair*, 2002. 5.5 x 11 x 6 (13.8 x 27.5 x 15 cm) and 9 x 8 x 5 in. (22.5 x 20 x 12.5 cm); white earthenware; pinched coil; hake and airbrushed terra sigillata; cone 06. Photo by artist.

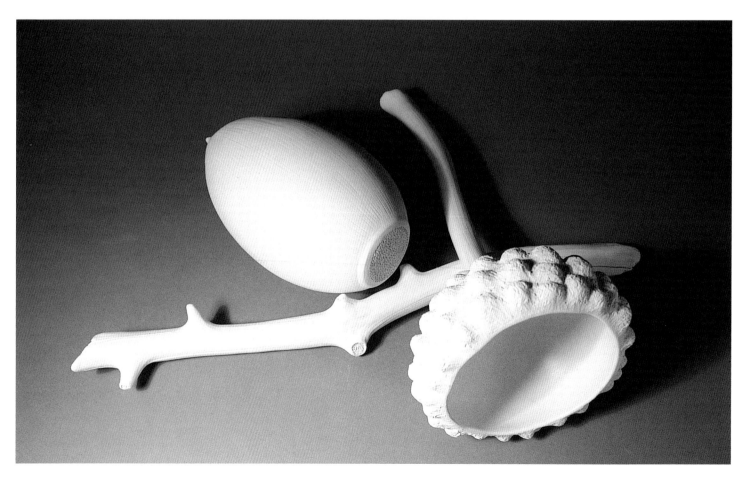

▲ *Acorn & Branch*, 2001. 2 x 2 x 25 in. (5 x 5 x 62.5 cm), 11 x 6.5 x 6.5 in. (27.5 x 16.3 x 16.3 cm), 8.5 x 8.5 x 19.5 in. (21.3 x 21.3 x 48.8 cm); white earthenware; pinched coil and extruded; brushed terra sigillata; cone 06. Photo by artist.

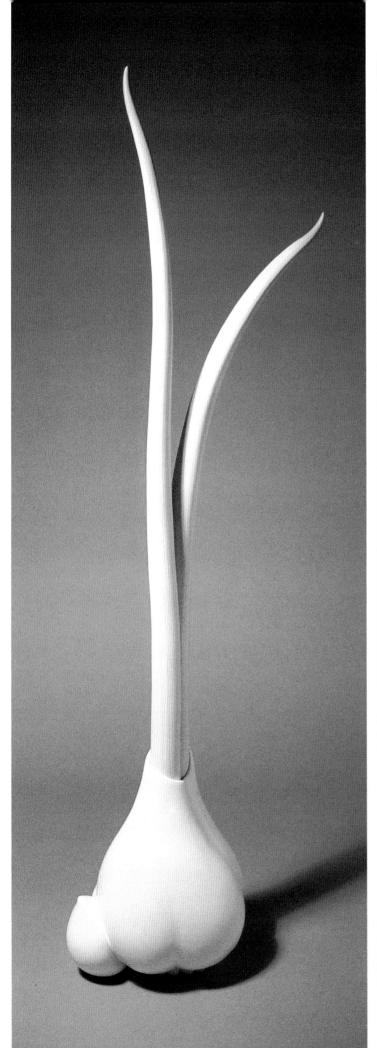

▲ *Hosta Trio*, 2001. 20 x 6 x 6 (50 x 15 x 15 cm),
23 x 6 x 6 (57.5 x 15 x 15 cm), 27 x 6 x 6 (67.5 x 15 x 15 cm); white
earthenware; slab and pinched coil; hake and airbrushed terra sigillata;
cone 06. Photo by artist.

◄ *White Onion VIII*, 2001.
36 x 8 x 7 in. (90 x 20 x 17.5 cm);
white earthenware; pinched coil and
extruding; hake and airbrushed terra
sigillata; cone 06.
Photo by artist.

SCULPTOR'S
Barn

This flexible clay space has an industrial

aesthetic well suited to Michael Sherrill's

large-scale ceramic-and-steel sculptures.

Tucked away in a wooded cove in Bat Cave, North Carolina, surrounded by rhododendron-covered mountains, is Michael Sherrill's enormous studio. Although its architecture resembles one, the 5,000-square-foot (450 m²) structure is a far cry from the old milk barn that served as his first studio when he was 17. Within this open, airy space, Michael has room for everything he needs to create his clay-and-steel sculpture.

Michael Sherrill's studio in Hendersonville, North Carolina

Michael's first concern in building the studio in 1999 was the structure's relation to the light and the land. After working on many possible designs and revisions, employing sophisticated architectural software, Michael actually liked his very first design best. It took professional builders (with some help from family members in the steel business) six months to complete construction of the studio on the property he'd owned for 16 years.

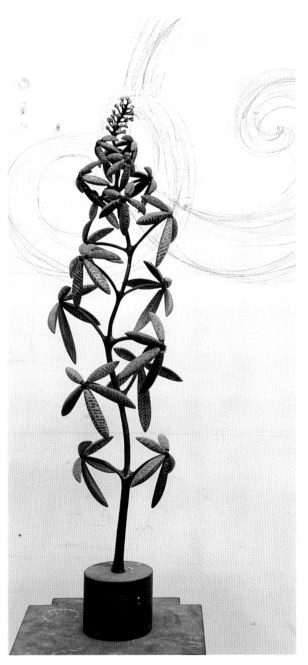

Maquette for the steel armature of a large commission

Michael often transforms nonclay objects or materials into useful tools.

The vast space of the studio, with its 26-foot-high (7.8 m) ceilings and open plan, is modeled after industrial shops and manufacturing plants. The wood-sided steel-beam structure stands on an unsealed concrete slab; he occasionally uses the studio floor to dry clay.

Naturally a shop of such proportions poses significant heating challenges. Greenhouse technology maximizes heat from a propane heater and a woodstove plus passive heat from a southern wall of windows and nighttime kiln firings. A clerestory, outfitted with electronically controlled airflow vents, dramatically breaks the roofline. Michael rolls up the truck-sized industrial doors during warm-weather months, flooding the studio with north light and bringing even more of the lush woods into view.

Metal fabrication equipment is located near the largest light source.

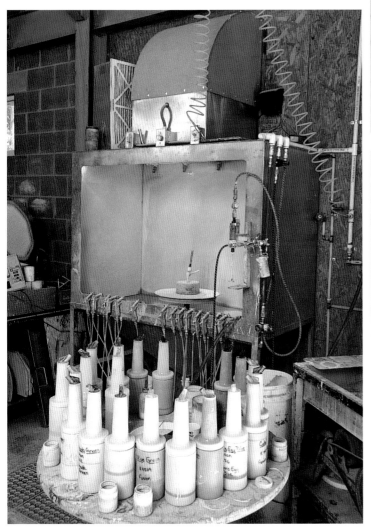

Both the waterfall spray booth and the airbrush equipment were modified by the artist.

The glaze area. A simple labeling and storage system keeps the process organized.

The impressive scale of the studio is perfectly suited to his equipment, processes, and finished work. There are dedicated spaces, which Michael refers to as "zones," for the work he creates in the two media, each of which requires its own tools and space. Welding and metal fabrication equipment stands in the clerestory, where the artist builds armatures for his sculptures. Michael's porcelain clay work centers around a pair of potter's wheels and a large power extruder, while wheeled cabinets hold dies and related equipment. Like his father before him, Michael is an inventor; he's redesigned the extruder and its dies, the spray glazing equipment, and other tools to suit his particular needs.

At the rear of the studio are areas for glazing, decorating, spraying, and firing. The work moves smoothly through Michael's elaborate coloring and firing processes. A large round table by the waterfall-style spray booth holds 20 plastic containers of colored slips. The computer-controlled electric kilns range along a fireproof masonry wall, and wheeled bisque racks stand nearby. Because he performs many rebisques of the same piece, he avoids kiln gasses by firing at night—as a bonus, the studio is warm the next morning. The artist forms, carves, and sands fired forms while sitting. He's given fresh life to several junkyard-salvaged steel workshop tables, reviving them with vibrant red paint, new wheels, and stainless tops. For ergonomic comfort, the heights of all work surfaces have been adjusted to suit Michael's own height and arm length. As he completes various parts for a sculpture, he fills his surrounding tables with them. A large mounted blackboard keeps his sketches, notes, and ideas available. Beyond the spray booth, at the studio's farthest reaches, are raw glazes and pallets of boxed clay (there's even a forklift). Michael often prepares and eats meals in the kitchen area; above it is a sleeping loft for guests. Michael's clay space is an unusual hybrid workshop put together to serve the needs of the mechanic and the engineer, the artist, and the inventor.

A table near the spray booth holds a glaze plan. A large area at the rear of the studio houses the largest and heaviest equipment.

The power extruder and all its related tools take up relatively little space.

Much of the studio's "furniture" has been adapted from other industrial applications. These salvaged industrial tables have durable new steel tops that are safe for many kinds of materials and are easy to clean.

Michael Sherrill studio
Hendersonville, North Carolina

This 5,000-square-foot (450 m²) studio design borrows from industrial and manufacturing structures. Its size, flexible space, and durable construction materials can handle any kind of job, from flameworking and metal fabrication to unloading clay with a resident forklift.

ABOUT THE ARTIST

Michael Sherrill is an autodidact who lives in Hendersonville, North Carolina. His work has appeared in numerous solo and group exhibitions in the United States. He's taught at many workshops, including the 92nd Street Y in New York, University of Nevada at Las Vegas, and El Camino College in Los Angeles. Michael's work is in the permanent collections of many museums, including The White House Collection of American Crafts and the Smithsonian American Art Museum's Renwick Gallery in Washington, plus a large number of well-regarded private collections. His work and studio have been featured in numerous catalogs, magazines, and books, including *The Penland Book of Ceramics* (Lark Books, 2003) and *Teapots Transformed: Exploration of an Object* (Guild Publishing, 2000). He recently installed a major commissioned piece in the plaza at First Union Bank in Charlotte, North Carolina.

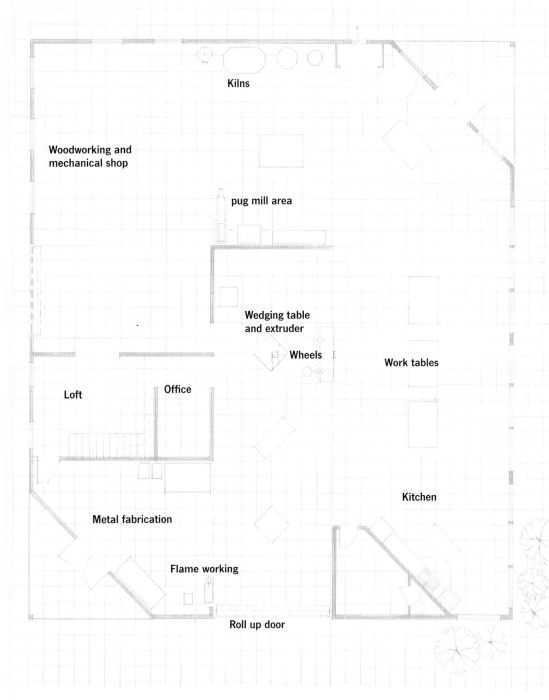

Kilns

Woodworking and mechanical shop

pug mill area

Wedging table and extruder

Wheels

Work tables

Loft

Office

Metal fabrication

Kitchen

Flame working

Roll up door

▸ *Junk Plant Beauty (Sumac)*, 2001. 32 x 32 x 32 in. (80 x 80 x 80 cm); carved porcelain; steel armature and glass head; abraded glaze; cone 6. Photo by Tim Barnwell.

◁ *October*, 2001. 14 x 14 x 10 in. (35 x 35 x 25 cm); carved porcelain; steel armature; abraded glaze; cone 6.
Photo by Tim Barnwell.

▲ *Seed*, 2001.
14 x 16 x 16 in. (35 x 40 x 40 cm); carved porcelain; steel armature; abraded glaze; cone 6.
Photo by Tim Barnwell.

◁ *She's Coming Out*, 2001.
14 x 21 x 11 in.
(35 x 52.5 x 27.5 cm); carved porcelain; steel armature; abraded glaze; cone 6.
Photo by Tim Barnwell.

TILE MAKER'S
Workspace

Kathy Triplett's modern space celebrates and uses the mountain landscape in delightful ways as she constructs her nature-inspired multi-part installations.

After working in 13 studios throughout her career, Kathy Triplett wanted to get off the beaten path. Her mountaintop ceramic studio is at the end of a winding, rutted road surrounded by breathtaking vistas of Western North Carolina valleys and ridgelines. The variety of clay studios she's inhabited—from a cramped basement in a rented house to a warehouse space in an artists' cooperative—honed her vision of the ideal rural studio where she could experience the beauty of natural morning light streaming into a high-ceilinged space. This location is perfect for her two passions: clay and gardening. A stone wall flanks the short lane from home to work space, and she confesses that the garden often seems like the reward for having spent the day in the studio.

The Triplett studio in Weaverville, North Carolina

Glaze test tiles form a mutable mosaic.

Kathy collects surfaces from the landscape.

Fresh air and passive solar heat circulate in from the greenhouse and out the clerestory vents.

Kathy and her husband designed the concrete block and wood-frame studio themselves, hiring a pair of professional carpenters (and two Croatian exchange students) to assist in the construction process. Workmen poured the cement slab and her husband built the block foundation. On-site poplar trees were milled at a neighbor's sawmill. The energy-saving structure uses clerestory windows for ventilation and has a south-facing glass greenhouse. The north wall is built into the mountainside.

The kiln room, located at the north end of the studio, will soon be separated from the work space by a block wall. The north-wall berm keeps the studio cool in the summer (unless the kilns are on) and holds kiln heat during the long, cold winters. The office and glaze-storage and kiln rooms can be closed off from the main room and left unheated, though Kathy also uses propane heat. There are four electric kilns of various sizes, since the artist fires finished work often and tests glazes every week. Her tiles have multifired layers of surface texture and color, so several kilns often operate simultaneously.

Wide wooden doors are one of four entrances to the studio.

Custom ceramic door handles adorn the barnlike studio doors.

The daily walk leads from house to garden to greenhouse.

The main work space is a single large room. Massive tree-trunk columns are reminders of the land on which the studio is built, and from them hang some of her most cherished tools. Equipment such as the slab roller and spray booth hugs the perimeter, while several sturdy wooden tables occupy the central space. A double-door entrance, which opens onto a stunning western view, is wide enough to drive a vehicle fully inside—especially handy in inclement weather. Although the windowed office can be accessed from within the studio, Kathy hopes to install a flagstone area just beyond its outside entrance and, to take advantage of the secluded location, perhaps an outdoor shower.

At Kathy's worktable, small boards of source design materials assist in the evolution of each element in the project.

The top shelf of a ware cart is used more for display than drying.

A beautiful poplar support column stands next to the hand-building table.

Plentiful stationary shelving space is all around the studio. High shelves that show off many of her colorful, animated teapots are an ingenious solution for display that doesn't steal space from the functional areas. Tables are moved to accommodate projects such as her wall installations, which Kathy often presents in large-scale grids. Her movements from one table to the next, arranging and assessing various groups of tiles, allow her to physically experience the flow of the developing project. Finished large projects are laid on the floor and photographed from above, a real time-saver. An area next to one of the columns, facing a western view of lush trees and ferns, is where the artist creates terra-cotta wall tiles from slabs she rolled the day before. Crucial to her comfort are thick, foam work mats on the floor around the slab roller and sculpting table; otherwise, the cement floor would tire her quickly. Kathy installed ceiling speakers for her CD player, since she feels that the workday doesn't really begin until the music does.

The view from the hand-building table encompasses artwork displays, the greenhouse entrance, and an amazing view.

Kathy considers herself a daytime artist, invigorated by the studio's streaming morning light and the greenhouse aromas that drift in. A typical day begins with an early morning walk through the garden, where she pulls weeds and looks for the newest blooms and sprouts. Often the excitement of opening a kiln gets her into work mode faster. She unloads it and examines the results, sometimes adding new glaze layers to the work for that evening's firing. Slabs rolled in the morning are ready for construction in the afternoon. Around four o'clock she and her two dogs take a brisk walk farther up the mountain, and it's this rhythm of work and home, by which Kathy is constantly renewed and informed, that has become her source of artistic inspiration.

Durable and inexpensive, canvas is a good cover for a wooden worktable.

In preparation for a workshop in Europe, Kathy practices her Italian whenever she can.

White walls show off Kathy's work best, and they can double as photo backgrounds.

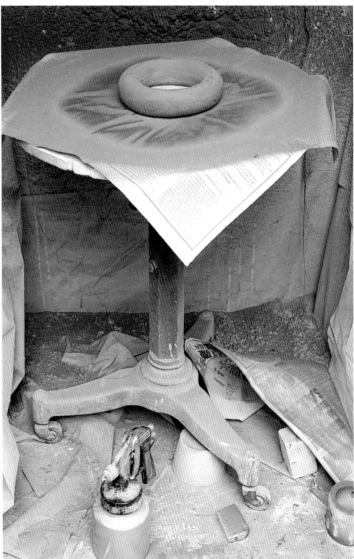

A homemade spray booth is fine, as long as it's properly vented.

Newspaper keeps a wooden worktable clean during glazing.

Kathy Triplett stands at her favorite spot.

The office is surrounded by cool green woods.

ABOUT THE ARTIST

Kathy Triplett lives in Weaverville, North Carolina, with her husband and two dogs, in a solar house filled with handmade tiles and ceramic wall sconces, and works in a hand-built studio nearby.

She attended the Universidad de las Americas in Pueblo, Mexico, and received a Bachelor of Arts degree from Agnes Scott College in Decatur, Georgia. Additionally, she has honed her artistic skills in courses at La Meridiana, Italy; Arrowmont School of Arts and Crafts, Tennessee; Castle Clay, Colorado; and the architecture department at Georgia Institute of Technology.

Though Kathy began her career as a potter, she now hand-builds with slabs and coils. She is the author of *Handbuilt Ceramics* (Lark Books, 1997) and *Handbuilt Tableware* (Lark Books, 2001) and has exhibited at Sculptural Object Fine Art (SOFA) New York and SOFA Chicago; First International Tokyo Crafts Expo in Japan; the American Craft Museum, New York; and is included in collections from Bolivia to Japan. She is a member of Piedmont Craftsmen and the Southern Highland Crafts Guild. She currently serves on the board of Handmade in America, in Asheville, North Carolina.

Kathy Triplett studio
Weaverville, North Carolina

This 1,320-square-foot (118.8 m²) workspace is simple, but flexible and focused.

The greenhouse measures 8 x 24 feet (.6 x 28 m)—big enough to start a garden.

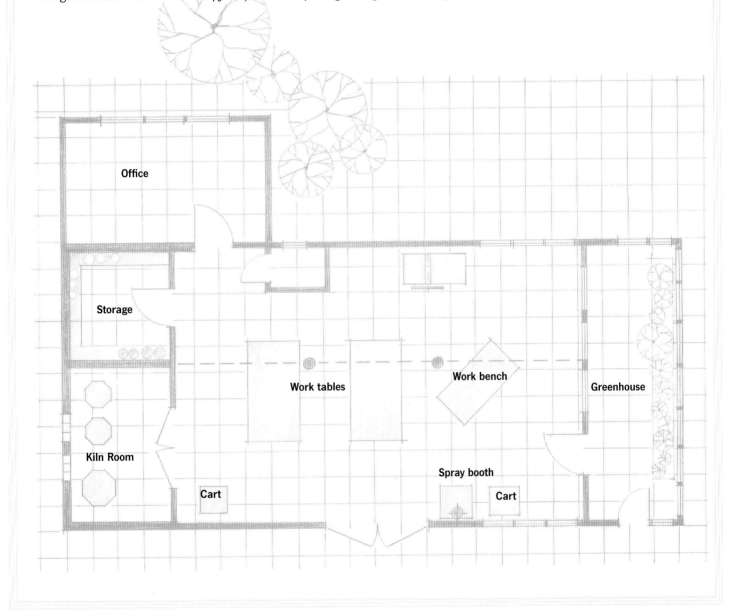

Kathy Triplett
GALLERY

▲ *The Garden After Sundown*, 1999. 30 x 90 x 3 in. (75 x 225 x 7.5 cm); clay; mixed media; hand built; glazes and stains; cone 03 and 3. Photo by artist.

▲ *Untitled*, 2002. 20 x 30 x 3 in. (50 x 75 x 7.5 cm); earthenware; slumped glass and mixed media; hand built; glazes and stains; cone 03. Photo by artist.

▶ *Untitled*, 2001, 30 x 20 x 3 in. (75 x 50 x 7.5 cm); earthenware; hand built; terra sigillata and stains; cone 03. Photo by Tim Barnwell.

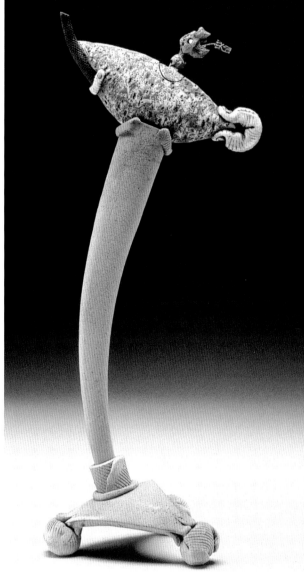

▲ *Lichen Tea*, 1999. 24 x 10 x 10 in.
(60 x 25 x 25 cm); clay; mixed media; hand built
and extruded; glazes and stains; cone 03.
Photo by Tim Barnwell.

▲ *Transformation*, 2001. 30 x 50 x 3 in. (75 x 125 x 7.5 cm);
earthenware; mixed media; hand built; glazes and stains; cone 03 and cone 3.
Photo by Tim Barnwell.

HAND BUILDER'S
House

Minimalist living space, studio quarters, and glaze house—every room in Mike Vatalaro's home and studio has wide, clear views that inspire his thrown-and-altered clay pieces.

Mike Vatalaro's glaze house and kiln pad is a short walk from the studio in his home.

Mike Vatalaro's clean, utilitarian, and flexible studio space embodies the practical beauty of the engineer. From the road his home appears to occupy only one story, but the property's open pastureland rolls enough for the structure to include a very large ground-level ceramic studio in the back. Both floors of the bi-level design include expansive, sky-filled views of the foothills of Pendleton, South Carolina.

The pureness of the space and lack of clutter inspire and focus this artist: "My work rhythm is influenced by empty tables. I fill the table with the forms I throw and on these large, open tables I explore the imaginative and creative process as I assemble thrown objects." The clay studio encompasses 1,650 square feet (148.5 m²)—far larger than the 10 x 12-foot (3 x 3.6-m) dining room that served as Mike's first studio. He developed the two-building design with a teaching colleague who's an architect.

Empty space spurs the creative process for Mike. The blackboard solution to the next construction is in a direct line with the table where the artist builds his pieces.

Still life with flyswatter

Mike sketches designs on a blackboard, sometimes pinning his thematically related monoprints alongside it. He arranged the angle of his electric wheel to a large window so that the broad side light fully sculpts the growing form and informs his creative process. He throws multiples of the future sculpture's various parts, which he later manipulates and joins to each other on a broad, canvas-covered table positioned under a large window. An adjoining room houses the office, a packing and shipping area, and finished pieces that stand on stationary shelving. The studio's sealed-concrete floor holds enough of the sun's heat to keep Mike comfortable through the short, mild winters, and grassy knolls are always in his line of sight.

Angled natural light best delineates the form as it takes shape on the wheel.

A collection of Mike's handmade and found wooden tools.

The foyer acts as a small gallery for his own work and collected pieces.

Mike Vatalaro's studio in Pendleton, South Carolina

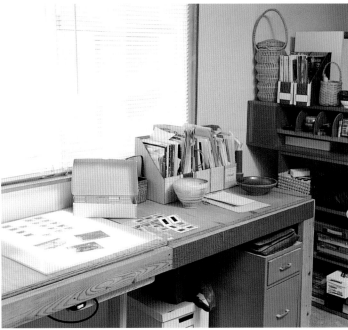

A lightbox built into a worktable in Mike's office makes good use of limited counterspace.

Stationary shelves work well in a storage room that is protected from exposure to most of the dusts and solutions of the studio.

Mike uses heirloom articles in the glaze house.

Plastic laminate countertops speed cleaning up glaze chemistry.

The same function-into-form principle is at work in the glaze house, where Mike executes the wetter parts of the process (spray glazing, clay mixing, and kiln firing). Many of the large pieces of furniture and equipment glide on wheels, including a car kiln that shares the small building's concrete pad. The casters save the artist's time and energy, and they work especially well on concrete. In the corner is a bench for metal fabrication, and two electric kilns are at the back wall. Mementos of his grandparents' lives (his grandmother's diminutive yard rake, the cup his grandfather used to dip homemade wine), along with clay's simpler hand tools, act as wall adornments. Even this quiet, tidy space has a sliding-glass-door view of the kiln and acres of prime horse country. At every turn Mike can drink in the beauty and spare function of space and landscape.

This homemade spray booth fits in a narrow space between wall and door where a manufactured unit couldn't.

Mike has a small workshop in the glaze house.

The protection for this outdoor kiln meets minimum airspace requirements for maximum safety and operation.

The clay mixer (on wheels, of course) rolls out from a small niche on the kiln pad.

On the kiln pad is an efficient storage unit for clay mixing materials.

A clay kitchen. Mike displays antique articles alongside everyday ones as a kind of wall installation.

Wheeled carts, dollies, and equipment lighten the heaviest work.

Mike Vatalaro in his studio

ABOUT THE ARTIST

Mike Vatalaro has lived in South Carolina and taught at Clemson University since 1976. Originally from Ohio, he received his B.F.A. in ceramics from the University of Akron.

In 1974 he attended New York State College of Ceramics at Alfred University, working with both wheel-thrown sculptural vessel forms and sculpture. He has been recognized in numerous regional and national shows and received the South Carolina Arts Commission Artist Fellowship in 1984 and 1993.
Mike has worked in a wide range of ceramic techniques and firing methods, most recently working with cone-10 reduction and soda kilns and constructing a 220-cubic-foot (6.6 m^3) anagama wood-fired kiln. He was included in the 2003 59th Scripps Ceramic Annual exhibition in Claremont, California.

Mike Vatalaro studio
Pendleton, South Carolina

Spacious and flexible, the artist's working space is suited to his creative process. The glaze studio, 150 feet (11.25 m) away from the house, holds the kilns, glazing and clay mixing equipment, and storage materials.

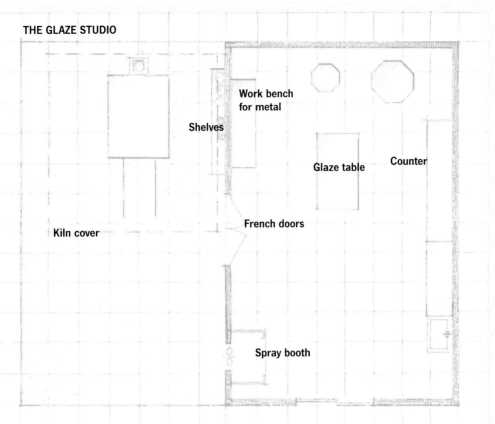

THE GLAZE STUDIO

Work bench for metal

Shelves

Glaze table

Counter

Kiln cover

French doors

Spray booth

Sliding doors

THE STUDIO

Work table

Work table

Wheel

Work table

Pin-up drawing wall

Work table

Shelving

Counter

▲ **Divided**, 2002. 9 x 21 x 21 in. (22.5 x 52.5 x 52.5 cm); stoneware; wheel thrown and assembled; slip with rutile wash; cone 10 reduction. Photo by Tim Barnwell.

▲ **Reconstructed Vessel**, 2000. 10 x 22 x 24 in. (25 x 55 x 60 cm); stoneware; wheel thrown and assembled; calcium satin matte; cone 10 reduction. Photo by Tim Barnwell.

▲ **Reconstructed Vessel**, 2001. 6 x 16 x 18 in. (15 x 40 x 45 cm); stoneware; wheel thrown and assembled; calcium satin matte; cone 10 reduction. Photo by Tim Barnwell.

▲ *Reconstructed Vessel*, 2001. 7 x 20 x 21 in. (17.5 x 50 x 52.5 cm); stoneware; wheel thrown and assembled; soda fired, cone 10. Photo by Tim Barnwell.

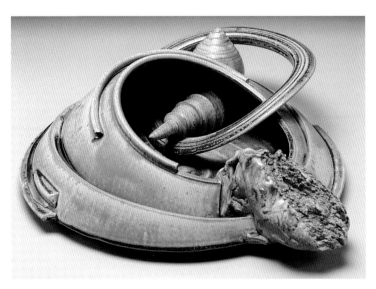

▲ *Crater*, 2001. 6 x 20 x 19 in. (15 x 50 x 47.5 cm); stoneware; wheel thrown and assembled; calcium satin matte; cone 10 reduction. Photo by Tim Barnwell.

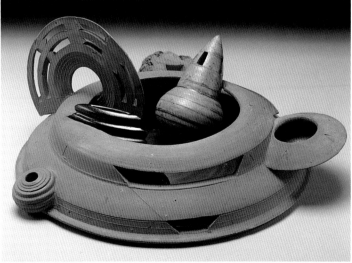

▲ *Harbor*, 2002. 9 x 21 x 20 in. (22.5 x 52.5 x 50 cm); stoneware; wheel thrown and assembled; rutile wash; cone 10 reduction. Photo by Tim Barnwell.

POTTER'S
Retreat

Cynthia Bringle's cozy clay space and gallery have been established for nearly three decades. Its comfortable sitting area welcomes visitors, students, and artists alike.

Cynthia Bringle is a potter and teacher who has mentored many of the ceramic artists living in the mountainous area of western North Carolina. In 1975 she built one of the first independent studios near Penland School of Crafts, a short distance from her house on a wooded hillside at the school's entrance. It's an evolving space that easily accommodates drop-in gallery traffic as well as any clay artist she might invite to make an extended stay. The welcoming atmosphere draws many people there to talk, work, and learn.

The Bringle studio very much reflects a steady evolution of work in wheel-thrown porcelain and stoneware pottery, which she high-fires in reduction and wood kilns. She also creates large-scale raku-fired slab work. Cynthia rented her first studio near Memphis, Tennessee, then worked for four years as a resident artist in a converted barn at Penland School before designing and building this one. From her early studio experiences she resolved to locate her studio in a community that supported fine craft (as well as the artists who create it), and over the years the space itself has acquired the look and feel of a long-established institution.

The gallery is cross-lit with natural light from a front window and its exterior access on the deck.

Finished work stands temporarily on the glaze table, while bisque work waits on carts for the next stage.

The light-filled, wood-beamed structure was designed with help from another Penland clay resident who was also an architect, and Cynthia oversaw the construction, which was done primarily by two carpenters. She first decided how much floor space she needed by measuring her resident artist space in the Penland Barns, adding in every direction to those dimensions, and making sure to also allow for storage, kiln, and showroom areas. There's a large central work space with pine flooring and a bi-level kiln pad. Off the main space, there's a showroom for finished work, a sitting area outfitted with a rudimentary kitchen and a stone fireplace, plus a guest loft for visiting ceramic artists.

The partially aboveground finished basement holds a propane-fueled heater to take the chill off and keep the pipes from freezing. Cynthia's original plan used ceiling-hung electric units for heat but she found them inefficient and expensive. Quick, cheery heat comes from the wood stove that was fitted into the original stone fireplace.

Natural light flows from three large 4 x 4-foot (1.2 x 1.2 m) skylights, but fluorescent fixtures are there for night work or gloomy days.

There's an impressive amount of work in progress here. Ware carts are full of pots in various stages of completion, from leather-hard to bisque to glaze. Facing double glass doors and a wall of windows is Cynthia's motorized kick wheel, with two tables and a wedging surface encircling it and a ware cart behind it. A treadle wheel stands nearby. From this central location, the work begins.

Instead of carrying bagged clay up from the basement storage space, Cynthia uses a dumbwaiter her brother installed in one corner of the studio—a real back saver. She throws, trims, and finishes construction on the raw clay from the wheel area, rolling full carts to the electric kilns for bisque firing, and using still more shelves and tables nearby for glazing. Ware carts move right onto the kiln pad, which holds a gas car kiln and, on a lower level, a single-chamber wood kiln and a raku kiln.

Cynthia's treadle wheel has an angle of view similar to that of the electric unit.

Fabricated-steel covers in the raku area of the kiln shed

Cynthia's tools move easily from electric to treadle wheels.

Ware carts brim with work ready for firing.

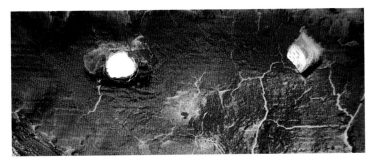

Peepholes in the wood kiln's door

Firing the catenary-arch wood kiln may take as long as 18 hours.
Task lighting lets Cynthia continue to work at night.

Cynthia thrives on stimulation from nature and visitors while she works. Since both her wheels face the sitting area and the windows, looking out to a handmade birdhouse on the wooden deck, Cynthia can throw, enjoy the wooded view and the birds, and chat simultaneously. She often collaborates with other artists, who may use the kitchen and sleeping loft over it to stay for extended periods of time.

The artist's compactly efficient gallery also offers many benefits. She keeps busy with commissions, and visitors to the gallery can see the full range of her work while she can get to know the people who buy it. This rural location receives high traffic in the summer months, and, similar to an open house, visitors are free to view the work even when Cynthia is busy elsewhere. In the gallery the artist sometimes spends a bit of quiet time with her own finished work.

The entire space has served Cynthia well over the past 28 years. She's made some minor renovations to her original plans, replaced the original aluminium-frame windows, and even replaced the roof, twice. Her kick wheel has seen a lot of pots and it's on its third motor. The studio is warm, open, lived in, and active. The moment you step in, it's apparent that she's a potter who lives to make pots and this hardworking studio allows her to share her talent and time with others.

The view from the kick wheel; the birdhouse was made by a friend of the artist.

Tools are ready near the wheel.

The sitting room's shelves hold ceramic pieces.

Storage shelves in the kiln shed

The glaze chemistry area

Kiln furniture on a rolling metal cart. The square kiln is a custom design.

The car kiln sits at the same level as the studio, while the catenary-arch wood kiln and raku areas are on a slightly lower level behind it.

The dumbwaiter is at the kiln end of the studio.

Cynthia Bringle in the studio with faithful companion, Pepper

ABOUT THE ARTIST

Cynthia Bringle makes functional wood-, salt-, gas- and raku-fired ceramic pieces—from mugs to vases to sink bowls—at her studio in Penland, North Carolina. She earned a Bachelor of Fine Art degree at Memphis Academy of Art in Tennessee and an M.F.A. at New York State College of Ceramics at Alfred University in New York. She has taught numerous workshops and exhibited for many years in the United States. Her work was featured in a one-person traveling exhibition in 1999, and resides in many private and public collections. She received the distinguished 2003 North Carolina Award for Fine Art.

Cynthia Bringle studio
Penland, North Carolina

The airy studio is 1,500 square feet (135 m²), with a sleeping loft over the gallery end. The bi-level, concrete-floored kiln area has raku, wood- and gas-fired kilns under a single roof

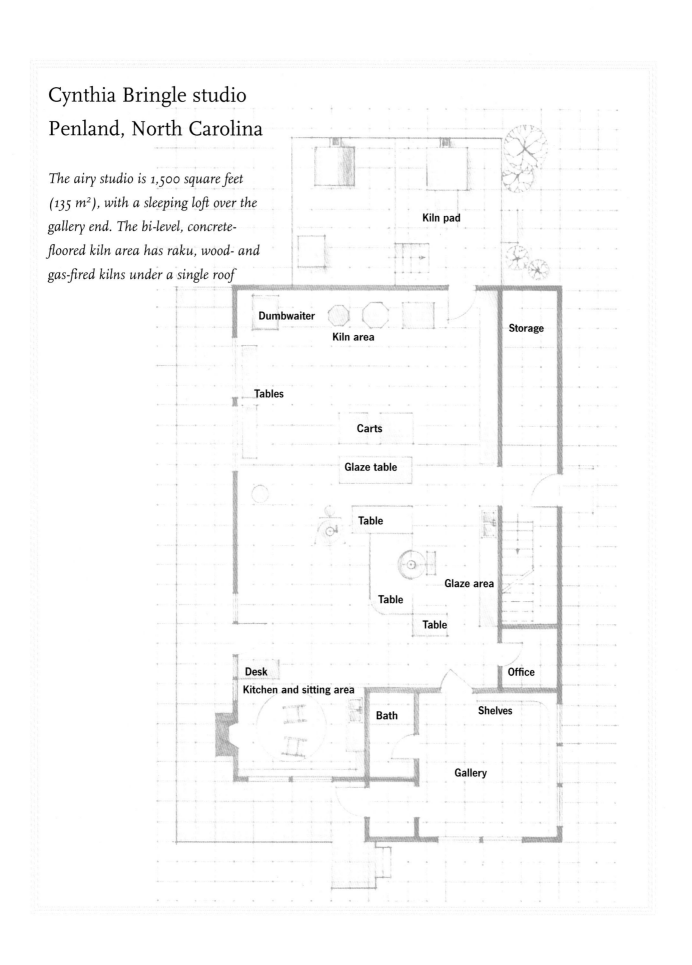

Kiln pad

Dumbwaiter

Kiln area

Storage

Tables

Carts

Glaze table

Table

Glaze area

Table

Table

Desk

Kitchen and sitting area

Office

Bath

Shelves

Gallery

⏷ **Goblets**, 2002. 6 x 7 in. (15 x 17.5 cm); stoneware; wheel thrown, carved, and faceted; gas kiln, cone 10. Photo by Tom Mills.

⏷ **Vase with Feet**, 2002, 9 x 7.5 in. (22.5 x 18.8 cm); porcelain; wheel thrown and ribbed; gas kiln, cone 10. Photo by Tom Mills.

⏷ **Pitcher**, 2002. 12 x 6 in. (30 x 15 cm); stoneware; wheel thrown and cut; salt fired in wood kiln, cone 10. Photo by m² photography.

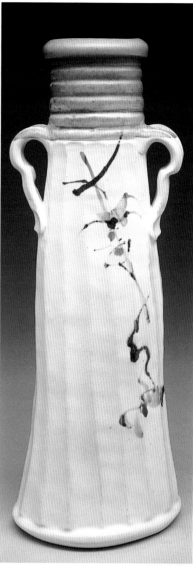

Vase with Handles, 2002. 12 x 3.5 in. (30 x 8.8 cm); porcelain; thrown and altered; gas kiln, cone 10. Photo by m² photography.

Teapot, 2002. 9 x 6 in. (22.5 x 15 cm); stoneware; wheel thrown and paddled; salt fired in wood kiln, cone 10. Photo by m² photography.

Platter, 2002. 20 x 4 in. (50 x 10 cm); stoneware; wheel thrown and folded; gas kiln, cone 10. Photo by m² photography.

Acknowledgments

The experience of writing this book at first seemed a daunting task. However, each memorable visit to the artists' studios renewed my desire and drive to work through the process.

I could not have written this volume without the enthusiastic cooperation of these 12 talented, dedicated, and inspiring artists: Cynthia Bringle, Debra Fritts, Becky Gray, Suze Lindsay, Kent McLaughlin, Alice Munn, Ben Owen III, Pam and Vern Owens, Michael Sherrill, Kathy Triplett, and Mike Vatalaro.

I also want to thank: David Ramsey, my dear friend and photographer extraordinaire; Suzanne Tourtillott, my editor, who kept me on task and offered inspirational encouragement and support at my weakest moments; Susan McBride, the art director, whose heartfelt vision helped me see the nuances and details in each studio; Bailey Ceramic Supply and Highwater Clays, whose employees provided technical support; and my husband, Peter Lenzo, and our three children, Tyler, Roxanne, and Joseph, who mostly give me unwavering love and encouragement.

Virginia Scotchie

About the Author

Virginia Scotchie is a ceramic artist and area head of ceramics at the University of South Carolina in Columbia, South Carolina. She holds a B.F.A. in ceramics from UNC–Chapel Hill and in 1985 completed her master of fine arts at the New York State College of Ceramics at Alfred University.

Virginia exhibits her work extensively throughout the United States and abroad, and has been awarded numerous artist residencies, including the Sydney Meyer Fund International Ceramics Premiere Award from the Shepparton Museum in Victoria, Australia. In 2003, she was one of 12 artists invited to participate in the prestigious 59th Scripps Ceramic Annual exhibition in Claremont, California. Her clay forms reside in many public and private collections, and articles and reviews about her continue to appear in well-known ceramics publications.

▲ *Pink Bowls,* 2002. 9 x 8 x 8 in. (3.5 x 3.2 x 3.2 cm) ea.; wheel-thrown and assembled; cone 6, oxidation. Photo by David H. Ramsey.

▲ *Three Avocado Forms*, 2002. 11 x 12 x 15 in. (4.3 x 4.7 x 5.9 cm) ea.; wheel-thrown and assembled; cone 6, oxidation. Photo by David H. Ramsey.

▲ *Two Black/Bronze Forms*, 2002. 8 x 14 x 15 in. (3.2 x 5.5 x 5.9 cm) ea.; wheel-thrown and assembled; cone 6, oxidation. Photo by David H. Ramsey.

▲ *Object Maker series*, 2002. ea. approx. 12 x 7 x 7 in. (4.7 x 2.8 x 2.8 cm); wheel-thrown and assembled; cone 6, oxidation. Photo by David H. Ramsey.

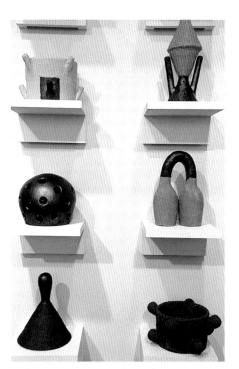

▲ *Pink/Bronze Form*, 2002. 8 x 6 x 6 in. (3.5 x 2.4 x 2.4 cm) ea.; wheel-thrown and assembled; cone 6, oxidation. Photo by David H. Ramsey.

▲ *Object Maker series* (detail), 2002. ea. approx. 12 x 7 x 7 in. (4.7 x 2.8 x 2.8 cm); wheel-thrown and assembled; cone 6, oxidation. Photo by David H. Ramsey.

Index